Jewish Personal Names

Their Origin, Derivation and Diminutive Forms

by Rabbi Shmuel Gorr ז״ל
Edited by Chaim Freedman

Avotaynu, Inc.
P.O. Box 99
Bergenfield, NJ 07621

Requests for permission to make copies of any part of this publication should be addressed to:

Avotaynu, Inc.
P.O. Box 99
Bergenfield, NJ 07621

Printed in the United States of America

Second Printing

Library of Congress Cataloging-in-Publication Data
Gorr, Shmuel
Jewish personal names: their origin, derivation and diminutive forms / Shmuel Gorr : edited by Chaim Freedman.
p. cm.
Includes indexes.
ISBN 0-9626373-2-7 (acid free paper)
1. Names, Personal—Jewish. 2. Names Personal—Yiddish. I. Freedman, Chaim. II. Title.
CS3010.G67 1992 929.4'4'089924043—dc20 92-24934

This book I dedicate to my dear mother Ḥayyah Sarah (may she be well and happy), who first revealed to me the world of the shtetl and from whom I first heard our traditional Jewish personal names.

"Because of four merits our ancestors were redeemed from the Egyptian bondage. They did not change their Hebrew names; they did not change their Holy Tongue (Hebrew); they did not change their Religion; nor did they change their specific Jewish clothing."

Rabbi Don Yitzḥak Abrabanel in his
Commentary to the Haggadah of Pesaḥ.

"In general, the NAME of a person determines one's destiny."

Babylonian Talmud, Berakhot, 7b.

Table of Contents

Foreword: Rabbi Shmuel Gorr ז״ל

This study of the diminutive forms and derivations of Jewish personal names was a labour of love over many years for the late Rabbi Shmuel Gorr. Whilst his interests in genealogy and Jewish history were many and varied, the subject of Jewish names was particularly close to his heart. Sadly, his untimely demise deprived him of the satisfaction of seeing his work published.

Shmuel Gorr was born in 1931 in Melbourne, Australia, to Russian immigrant parents who both stemmed from many generations of eminent rabbis, in particular, the Maharal of Prague. At the age of fifteen, he was the first Australian youth sent to study at Telz, a prominent overseas Yeshiva in the USA. He furthered his studies at Gateshead Yeshiva in England before returning to Australia. Upon completion of his studies, he received Semikha (rabbinic ordination).

Whilst managing his late father's business, Rabbi Gorr managed to lead an active communal and intellectual life in Melbourne. He studied history, art and comparative religion and lectured on Jewish art at Melbourne and Monash Universitieswhere he was a counsellor for Jewish students. In 1961, he founded the Ben-Uri Art Museum and was its director until 1968. He was art critic for the Jewish press in Melbourne and wrote a number of books of his own poetry and prose that reflect the depth of his philosophy of Jewish existence.

In 1968, Rabbi Gorr emigrated to Israel settling in his beloved Jerusalem. He worked for and contributed articles to the *Encyclopedia Judaica* until 1973. In that year he served with the Israel Defense Forces in the Yom Kippur War. In 1974, he founded an archive of 16,000 photographs of rabbis of many communities over the last two hundred years. This led him to his interest in genealogy and Jewish history in general.

Rabbi Gorr contributed articles to a wide range of journals both in the field of genealogy and Jewish life in general. In 1976, he was editor of the religious magazine *Shema Yisrael* and in 1978, of *The Light*. He was a contributing editor of *Search*, an international journal of Jewish genealogy. His articles appeared in Hebrew in the Israeli orthodox press, in particular *Hamodiah*.

In the course of his researches, Rabbi Gorr visited the United States, Australia and New Zealand and lectured there. In 1982, he was "Scholar in Residence" at the Second Summer Seminar on Jewish Genealogy held in Washington, DC, and likewise at the fourth seminar in Chicago in 1984. He also lectured to a wide range of organisations including Yeshiva students, women's groups and Jewish cultural organisations.

The subject of the Holy Land and its settlement by Jews in the nineteenth century was particularly dear to him and bound him body and soul to Jerusalem. He became intimately familiar with the last resting place of those Jews whose yearning for the Holy Land brought them to the Jewish Cemetery on the Mount of Olives. He developed special techniques for locating, restoring and photographing old tombstones.

Rabbi Gorr was commissioned from time to time by Yad Ben Tsvi, Yad Vashem, Keter Publishing and other institutions to prepare special research projects, but his prime love was the personal genealogical research which he carried out for thousands of clients over a period of twenty years. Not only did Shmuel Gorr gain a reputation as one of the leading Jewish genealogists, but he established warm personal relationships with his many clients and contacts in all walks of Jewish life.

Blessed with an intuitive skill in tracing rare sources, Shmuel Gorr amassed a private collection of printed texts and copies of manuscripts. He prepared thousands of family trees based on these sources and on information provided by his clients. He had a phenomenal memory for sources, and his colleagues could always be confident of receiving sound advice on where to further their research.

Shmuel Gorr was a fascinating, if not eccentric, character. He kept open house for a never-ending stream of colleagues, friends and clients. His marathon telephone conversations across the country, his tenacity in seeking out far-flung leads to sources, his vibrant enthusiasm to preserve every last link in the chain of Jewish existence, all were integral facets of his personality. He was a familiar figure in Jerusalem, and, as he walked the streets downtown, he would be greeted by acquaintances on nearly every corner. He always found time for anyone requiring his help, and his total physical and mental dedication to his work was to exact a heavy price on his health.

Shmuel Gorr was a staunch adherent of Chabad, revering its leader the Lubavitcher Rebbe to whom he often turned for advice. In fact, he obtained special permission from the Rebbe to dedicate his life to research rather than pursue a more traditional scholastic career. Shmuel Gorr radiated a love of Yiddishkeit which was the driving force behind his researches. He believed that the conducting of research into one's family and ancestry was a holy task and mission. In a learned treatise based on traditional religious sources, he concluded that just as we perform certain rituals and observe festivals, 'Zekher lemaase Bereishit' (in remembrance of the Act of Creation), so the discovery of the links in the long chain of Jewish existence was "yet another affirmation of faith in the act of creation of the world by God."

Rabbi Shmuel Gorr's untimely death on Elul 21, 5748 (September 3, 1988) left an irreplaceable void for his many friends and colleagues. He was involved in the compilation of a number of books stemming from his researches, but none reached completion. It is hoped that this work will be the forerunner of others and that Shmuel Gorr's contribution to Jewish scholarship will be thus available to a wider public.

As this book was published after his death, it was decided to present it in the form he wrote with minimal editorial corrections.

Chaim Freedman
Petah Tikvah, Israel
1992

Acknowledgements

We wish to thank the family of the late Rabbi Shmuel Gorr for providing the manuscript for this book. Jane Freedman, my wife, spent numerous hours coding the Hebrew text to make it possible to encode the data in a English-language word processing system. Gary Mokotoff provided the typographical design of the book and Rose Marie Ciecierski keyboarded the manuscript.

Introduction

What word, more than any other, stirs a person to immediate reaction? What word normally stays with one throughout one's life? What word consciously or otherwise means the most to one? One's name. Once given a name at birth, one becomes identified with that name. If one is called by one's name and the name is mispronounced, it is immediately corrected. A person feels uneasy when his/her name is mispronounced. It is almost as if one's being has been violated.

But how many of us know the real meanings of the names we carry all our lives, those which are engraved on our tombstones and bestowed on our descendants? Today, the old query, "What's in a name?" carries a more dramatic urgency.

One of the most disturbing phenomenon regarding the naming of Jewish children is the fact that even in cases where traditional sentiment demands the perpetuation of names of our dear departed ones, we force our children to live the lives of Crypto-Jews. Those who never received Jewish names—theirs is the greater tragedy.

The vicissitudes of history have allowed assimilation to cause Jewish names, in cases where they have been given, to be used in a manner not unlike at meetings of secret societies. Who would suspect that *Gary* is really (in some cases) the transposition of *Tzvi Herschel*—the "Herschel" being pronounced "Gershel" in Russia, and on migrating to a Western country, the "Gary" was selected as being least obvious as a Jewish derivative? Quite an amazing feat! But do we need such acrobatics? Why not just simply Tzvi, or Tzvi Herschel, or Herschel?

When a Jew is called to the reading of the Torah, he is called up by his full Hebrew/Yiddish name, but on a regular basis, he is known by his non-Jewish name. There are many strictly orthodox Rabbis who are also guilty of this crypto-style existence. What kind of a name for an orthodox Rabbi is Harav *Irving* Critton? In truth, his name is Harav *Yisrael* Kritchevski.

Much has been, and much could be, written on this subject, but let these few lines suffice to jar our fellow Jews into giving, living with, and using in everyday life, their traditional Jewish names. They are surely not embarrassed to carry and be known by a name of a progenitor or other relative. Thus, they would truly perpetuate the dead person's memory, thereby, making all the past generations live in him or her.

Our intention in this small handbook is to elucidate the origins and meanings of as many Jewish names as is possible. This small work is not intended to be for the specialist, nor exclusively for the trained scholar; rather, it is an attempt to share with fellow Jews and Jewesses the results of my research into the origins, form-developments and eventual diminutive forms of many Jewish names.

The indexed listing, provided later in this work, is not exhaustive, and with the Almighty's help, it may eventually turn out to be the preview to a larger and more in depth research.

Unfortunately, the origins and meanings of many male, and even more Jewish female, names are probably lost forever, but we have managed to salvage many.

Too many untrained people have surmised and guessed at the basis of folk etymology to interpret Jewish names. The damage caused thereby is that contemporary Jews who do want to have and use Jewish names have, through lack of knowledge, Hebraised them incorrectly. One example should suffice: The Jewish female name *Fruma* or its older form which still exists, *Frumet*, does not mean "a pious one." It is a female name adopted by Jews from medieval France and in its original form was *Fromentine*, a species of black grapes. The modern Hebraising to *Hassidah* is absolutely incorrect. The true meaning having been lost for hundreds of years, caused the mistake of misidentity of the name to occur.

A few guidelines in the use of this book is in order. Jews and Jewesses use Hebrew, Yiddish and Yiddishised names.

This work will not deal with the myriad non-Jewish names adopted or used by Jews during the last 150 years. As this has no bearing on the matter at hand, only those Yiddish names that were of old and traditionally adopted from non-Jewish sources and preserved exclusively by Jews, will be dealt with.

Let us now enumerate the basic categories of traditional Jewish names:

1. a) Hebrew
   b) Aramaic
   c) Yiddish
   d) Non-Jewish
2. Translations of those in Group 1.
3. Diminutives and double diminutive forms of both Groups 1 and 2:
   a) Old High German.
   b) German. Different local forms.
   c) Slavic—Russian, Polish, etc.
4. Abbreviations of all above groups.
5. Phonetic derivation.

In addition to these categories, we must bear in mind a few basic facts concerning linguistics and phonetics. First, we should not lose sight of the fact that the course of European Jewish migration from the Iberian Peninsula (Spain and Portugal) through France and Holland to Central Europe climaxed in an eventual redeployment in East European countries. Jewish phonetics were influenced at each stopover.

The languages of influence involved include Old Castillian (Spanish) and Old French; Old High German and its various dialects; and finally, the Slavic language group. A minor influence came from Italy. These language groups are in many ways exclusive. To illustrate: Some Slavic language speakers do not have the simple aspirate *H*, and it ends up as a *G* (i.e. *H*urewitz becomes *G*urewitz).

No person or group of persons are immune to the phonetical influences of their host country. This is obviously true of Jewry. Just look at the variations of Hebrew and Yiddish pronunciations: Shmuel and Shmiel, Moshe and Meishe, and even Fruma and Frima, or Frume and Frime.

Many of you will recall that you learned at school the breakdown of the phonetics of our consonants and vowels. But it is imperative for us to keep these rules in mind if we are to successfully research our subjects. Hence, these rules are laid out here as a reminder.

Chart I

1. Labial = lips
   a) Bi-labial - P, B, W.
   b) Labio-dental - F, Ph, V.
2. Dental = teeth
   T, D, M, N, L, R, Th, S, Sh, Z, Zh, Ch, (as in cheese)
   Ts, Tz, Cs, Cz.
3. Palatial = roof of mouth
   Y.
4. Velar = soft part of palate
   K, G, Ng.
5. Glottal = vocal chords
   H, Ch. (as in the Scottish Lo*ch*).

Chart II

Phonetically Interchangeable Consonants

B	B - P
D	D - T
F	F - Ph - V
I	I - Y
K	K - G
M	M - N
P	P - B
S	S - Sh - Z - Zh
T	T - D
V	V - F - Ph - W
W	W - V - F - Ph
X	Kh
Z	S - Sh - Z - Zh

Getting back to our basic categories of traditional Jewish names, it may be in order to take one example from each one to demonstrate the processes involved.

The Hebrew boy's name Zeev is very commonly coupled with the German translation "Wolf," and we end up with original and translation—Zeev Wolf. For reasons outside the scope of this book, the Wolf became the dominantly used name. Some European languages have a problem with what we would consider a simple *w*, and they pronounce it *v*. (Think of our immigrant grandparents who continued to say "vot do you vont" instead "what do you want.")

Hence, a remarkable transformation happened to many Jewish names in Slavic countries. A simple Germanic (by now, read: Yiddish) name like Wolf turned into Velvel. Who would suspect that Velvel was actually Zeev? Let us analyse what happened.

Zeev in Germanic translation becomes Woolf. In one of the Germanic dialectical diminutive forms, Woolf becomes Woolf*el*. Another phonetical influence turns the *w* into *v*, and hence Voolf, and in diminutive form Voolf*el*. As shown in Chart II, the *f* also can change into a *v*, and so in Slavic-speaking countries Voolf*el* becomes Vool*vel*, and by phonetic influence of the vowels, we end up with a majestic Velvel.

In this example, we have shown how a Hebrew male name is used in Germanic translation and two local developments of its diminutive forms.

Let us now illustrate a female Jewish name. We shall demonstrate the process of abbreviation. Everyone knows the Hebrew woman's name *Yehudit*. A simple contemporary diminutised abbreviated form is *Ditty*. But let us tackle a traditional form. One of the major Slavic language diminutive suffices is the *k*, *ke* or *ka* (like Fruma = Frum*ka*).

One abbreviated form of Yehud*it* is *I*tte or *I*tta. With a Slavic language diminuitive suffix it becomes *I*tke or *I*tka. To compound the issue, we have the Hebrew female name *Esth*er. In the abbreviated form it becomes *Ett*a or *Ett*e, and with the added Slavic language diminutive suffix, it becomes *Et*ka or *Et*ke. Because the *E* is a soft or weak letter, we can have it pronounced also as an *I*, and we end up with *It*ka or *It*ke. Hence, in this case, one has to be very careful in seeking the original name, starting with Itka or Itke. Etka or Etke would most probably go back to Esther, but watch the *It*ka or *It*ke.

To make this handbook less complicated and of maximal aid to those using it, I have endeavored to simplify the search. Hence, I have listed all variant forms and spellings of all the names included herein, alphabetically. Where the originals are pure Hebrew names, I have not translated them. Others have already created major works on the subject. For all Aramaic, Yiddish and non-Jewish names, I have endeavored to supply not only all variations of abbreviated and diminutive forms, but also their translations or original meanings.

There must be mentioned another important directive. The two major Old Germanic diminutive suffixes were *el* or *le*, and *man(n)*. Another German language diminutive suffix is *del*. It usually follows a name ending in *n*. To give a few examples: Shein*del*, Min*del*, Brein*del*, and strange though it may be, Men*del*, which developed from *Men*aḥem Mann. *Mann* is an abbreviation of *Men*aḥem, and in this diminutive form, it become Men*del*—hence the popular name Menaḥem Men*del*.

The major Slavic diminutive suffix was *ke* or *ik*, and there even exists such a form as a double diminutive suffix, i.e. Shmuel—Shmuel*ke*—Shmuel*kele*. A less common diminutive suffix hailing from Poland, Galicia, Hungary and Roumania is *ush* or *ish*, i.e. Ber–Ber*ish*, Abba–Abb*ush* or Abb*ish*, and Dobra–Dobr*ush* or Dob*ish*, Benyomin–Bein*ush* or Bein*ish*.

An older Germanic diminutive suffix is *lin* which derived from *lein*. An abbreviated diminutive form of the male name Yisrael is Isser. A remarkable form developed—the diminutive became Isserel—and from that form, the diminutive became Isserlein and finally Isserlin. This last form also was adopted as a family name.

Let us not forget that a diminutive form of a name is a display of affection meaning "dear one" or "little one." An example taken directly from the German language will be the best demonstration. In German an adult or married woman is called Frau, and a young or unmarried woman is called Frau*lein*.

For as long as is recorded, Ashkenazi Jews normally do not name a child after a living relative. Most Sephardim have no inhibitions in naming a son after a living relative—even after a living father. A son or daughter who was born after the death of the father or mother would usually be named after the respective dead parent. Hence, even an Ashkenazi child could carry the identical name of his parent.

Certain names were once carried by either of the sexes, but today, especially amongst Ashkenazi Jews, these names have become polarized to one sex only. Long ago, the name Simḥa was used by both Ashkenazi men and women. Today, amongst Ashkenazi Jews, Simḥa is almost exclusively a male name. There exists, however, a female derivative diminutive form—Sim*a*.

A basic rule of most diminutive forms of Jewish personal names is that once these names are born, they leave home and become independent. Even an Ashkenazi Jew named Simḥah would have no compunction in naming his daughter Sima. Another interesting point is that although the Yiddish translation or equivalent of both Yehudah and Aryeh is Leib, even Ashkenazi Jews could name a son Yehuda ben Aryeh or Aryeh ben Yehudah.

Pronunciation Guide

		As In:	Example:
Vowels:	a	last	Bluma
	e	bed	Esther
	i	ink	Elisha
	o	hot	Dov
	u	full	Fruma
Dipthongs:	ai	Thailand	Shamai
	ei	shein	Freida
	ie	lieber	Lieberman
	ol	poise	Efroiyim
Consonants:	ḥ	loch	Hayyim
	kh	Khartoum	Barukh
	tz	blitz	Tzeitel
	cz	Czechoslovakia	Czarne
	zh	measure	Drozhna

Shmuel Gorr ז´´ל
Elul 5743
August 1983

Additional Introductory Notes by the Editor

This book is arranged such that the main body of text contains the root Hebrew names from which the derivatives and diminutive forms arose. Each derivative is given with all forms of Yiddish/Hebrew spelling that were located by the author. The English names are transliterations of the Yiddish/Hebrew; therefore, a familiarity with Hebrew script is an advantage. It should be born in mind that traditional Yiddish spelling differs from Hebrew with respect to pronunciation of vowels and certain consonants. In general, the Yiddish form follows Ashkenazic pronunciation and not that of modern Hebrew which is the Sephardic.

In addition to the pronunciation guide to the English text given by the author, it is necessary to understand Yiddish spelling conventions which are the basis for the English transliteration, the latter having no basis in its own right.

The following principles need to be noted:

אָ = o
אַ = a
ט = t
ת = s[1]
תּ = t[2]
לֶע = le[3]
בֵיי = bey[4]

(1) Hebrew form pronounced *t* in the Sephardi form or *s* in the Ashkenazi form.

(2) Dotted Hebrew form pronounced *t* by both Ashkenazim and Sephardim. Rarely used in Yiddish where replaced by ט.

(3) Sound conveyed by placing the vowel under the consonant proceeding the ע.

(4) Sound conveyed by placing the vowel under the consonant preceding two י.

There are two schools of thought as to the combination of consonants and vowels which indicate a particular sound. In the author's original text the sound לֶע (*le*) is spelled לעֶ. These corrections have been made in accordance with the majority of Yiddish texts. Since most Yiddish texts have no undervowelling anyway, this issue is left to conventional understanding of the consonant indicating the sound.

Indexes: The personal name index not only enables the location of all forms covered in the text, but is a handy reference for establishing which root names were their source. The list of family names further broadens the scope of this book, since it not only includes those surnames referred to in the text, but adds many others which are also derived from the personal names.

Male Personal Names

Aharon (Aron) אהרן

Biblical. Shemot, 4:14, 6:20.
From the root אוֹר (light). Indicating the holy task of Aharon, the High Priest, in lighting the menorah in the Sanctuary in the desert. Also, from הוֹרָאָה (teaching—enlightening). Aharon was the great peace maker.

Aron[1]	אַרוֹן[1]
Oren	אָרֶען
Ore	אָרֶע
Arel	אַרֶעל
Arele	אַרֶעלֶע
Orel	אָרֶעל
Arke[1a]	אַרְקֶע[1a]
Orke[1b]	אָרְקֶע[1b]
Arush[1c]	אַרוּשׁ[1c]
Orush	אָרוּשׁ
Arushka	אַרוּשְׁקַא
Arushke	אַרוּשְׁקֶע

1. The weak ה is elided.
1a. The family name *Arkin* derives from this form. See also footnote 9.
1b. The family name *Orkin* derives form this form.
1c. *Ush*, *ash*, *ish*, and *esh* are diminutive suffixes, being a softening of the Germanic *ch* and *che.*

Aleksander[2] (Alexander[3]) אלכסנדר[3, 2]

Old Greek. Alexandros.
"A helper of men" — "Defender."

Aleksender	אַלֶעכסַאנדֶער
Aliksender	אַלֶעכסֶענדֶער
Sender	אַלִיכסַאנדֶער
Sander[4]	אַלִיכסֶענדֶער
Sandor	סַאנדֶער
Sender'l	סֶענדֶער
Sendush[4a]	סַאנדוֹר
Sandush	סֶענדֶערֶעל
	סַאנדוּשׁ[4a]
	סֶענדוּשׁ

2. Very often coupled with *Ziskind*. Reason unknown.

3. Adopted for use by Jews in honour of Alexander the Great because of his benevolent treatment of the Jews during his military campaign to conquer the world.
4. This form was so close to the non-Jewish family name that many Jews whose father's and grandfather's name was *Sander*, simply adopted the surnames *Sanders* or *Saunders* after migrating to English-speaking countries. *Alexander* also became a family name.

4a. See footnote 1c.

Alter[5] אַלטֶער[5]

German.
"Old one." In Yiddish, an "old man." One of the amuletic names.

Alter	אַלטר
Altir	אַלטֶער
Altmann[6]	אַלטִיר
	אַלתר
	אַלתֶער
	אַלתִיר
	אַלטְמַאן[6]
	אַלטְמַן

5. This is one of the amuletic names. If a male child died soon after birth or very young, the next born male child was sometimes given the name *Alter* alone, or in combination with another name. The parents, in giving the name, expressed their prayer that the newborn child should live to be an *old* man. See also *Alte*. The family name *Alter* is a derivative.*
6. See footnote 36. This diminutive also developed into a family name.

* Not to be confused with the family name *Altar* which has a completely different etymological origin. *Altar* was a small island in a river in medieval France. After a local pogrom, some Jews who escaped adopted the name of their place of birth as their family name.

Aryeih (Aryeih Leib) אריה

Biblical. Bereishit, 49:9.
"Lion." Indicating strength, and fearlessness. Yehudah took the lion as the symbol of his Tribe, and as Jerusalem became the capital of the Kingdom of Yehudah, the lion is the symbol of the City of Jerusalem.

Leib[7]	לֵייבּ[7]
Leibel	לֵיבּ
Leibele[7a]	לֵייבֶּעל

Leibish[7b]	לייבעלע[7a]
Leibush	לייביש[7b]
Lev	לייבוש
Levke	לעוו
Aryeh	לעווקע
Ari'[8]	ארי'[8]
Arik	אריק
Artze	ארצע
Artzi	ארצי
Arke[9]	ארקע[9]
Arel[9]	ארעל[9]

7. *Leib* is Yiddish for "lion," and as the symbol of the Tribe of Judah is a lion, *Leib* is used also together with the name *Yehudah*. See also *Yehudah Leib.**

7a. *The* family name *Leibler* derives from this form. From the old Judeo-German (early Yiddish) forms *Löwe* and *Löbl*, there were derived the names *Loew* and *Loebel—Lobel*.

7b. See footnote 1c.

8. The Hebrew letters י and ה together form a name of God. To avoid writing, and possibly pronouncing, God's name, an apostrophe took the place of the final ה in writing.

9. It is bound to happen that diminutives of more than one Hebrew/Yiddish name end up being phonetically identical. This is the result of Yiddish phonetics. See *Aharon*—diminutive, *Arel* and *Arke*.

* In certain countries, Jews with the name *Aryeh* or *Yehudah* used other translations such as *Leon* and *Leo*. From these translations there developed the family names *Leeman* and *Lehman*. See footnote 3. Not to be confused with the family name *Leiman*, a derivative of *Lemu'eil*.

Asher[10, 11] אשר[10, 11]

Biblical. Bereishit, 30:13.
"Happy one." Son of Zilpah, handmaid of Lei'ah, wife of Yakov. On Asher's birth Lei'ah proclaimed, "For my happiness; for daughters will call me happy. And she called his name Asher." Father of the Tribe carrying his name.

Osher	
Osherel	אשרל
Osher'l	אשרעל
Asherel	אנשעל
Asher'l	אנשיל
Anshel (Anschel)	אנזעל[13]
Anshil (Anschil)	אנזיל

Anselm[12]	ענזעל
Anzel[13]	ענזיל
Anzil	ענזלין
Enzel	הענזעל[14]
Enzil	הענזיל
Enzlin	זעליג[14a]
Henzel[14]	זעליק[14a]
Henzil	זעליגמאן[14b]
Zelig[14a]	זעליקמאן
Zelik[14a]	זעלע
Zeligman[14b]	
Zelikman	
Zelle	

10. Often combined with Lemel. Reason unknown. See footnote 79.
11. *Asher* is very often combined with its Yiddish (read Judeo-German) translation *Zelig*. Amongst Jews, the practice of combining the Hebrew and Yiddish (translation) names as one was very common, and in daily use the Yiddish translation was used more often.
12. The Old High German name *Anselm* was so close to the Yiddish diminutive *Ans(c)hel* that presumably German-speaking Jews felt at ease with *Ans(c)hel*.
13. שׁ and ז are both dentals, and therefore interchangeable.
14. Just as the ה is very often elided, the dynamics of phonetics sometimes adds the ה where it basically does not belong. *Henzel* and *Henzil* became family names. As mentioned in the previous footnote, שׁ and ז are interchangeable, hence *Henschel* (*Henshel*) is also a derivative family name.
14a. The German (hence Yiddish) translation of *Asher*. As *k* and *g* are both of the velar group, *Zelig* also developed into *Zelik*.
14b. Both forms became family names. See footnote 36. *Seelig*, *Seligman* and *Zelikman* are phonetic variations of the same names. See footnote 70.

Avraham (Abraham) אברהם

Biblical. Bereishit, 17:5.

Originally the name was *Avram*, which means "exalted father." In his commentary on Bereishit 17:5, Rashi, the great Biblical and Talmudic commentator, explains that the earlier form of the name indicates that he was the spiritual father to *Aram* and his people, the Arameans from whence Avraham hailed. The Almighty added the letter ה to his name and it became Avra*h*am. The new name inferred that Avraham thus became the spiritual "father of a multitude of nations." The ה is the key letter in the Holy name of God. Avraham was the pillar of hospitality. Tradition tells us that his tent opened on all four sides in order to make it easier for wayfarers to enter and receive hospitality. Progenitor of the Jewish People.

Avram[15]	
Avrom	אַבְרָם[15]
Avremel	אַבְרֶעמֶעל
Avremele	אַבְרֶעמֶעלֶע
Avremka	אַבְרֶעמקַא
Avremke	אַבְרֶעמקֶע
Abba	אַבַּא
Abbale[16]	אַבַּאלֶע[16]
Abbele	אַבֶּעלֶע
Abish[16a]	אַבִּישׁ[16a]
Abush	אַבּוּשׁ
Abrasha[16a]	אַבְרַאשַׁא[16a]
Abrashe	אַבְרַאשֶׁע
Abrashka	אַבְרַאשקַא
Abrashke	אַבְרַאשקֶע
Avrel	אַבְרֶעל
Avril	אַבְרִיל
Eivril[17]	עֵבְרִיל[17]

15. The *h*, or more correctly, the ה of the Hebrew alphabet, is phonetically a weak letter, and hence, in speech is elided.
16. The family names *Abeles*, *Abelesz*, etc. derive from these forms.
16a. See footnote 1c.
17. *Avraham Eiver* is a two name combination which is still in use. The diminutive of *Eiver* is *Eivril*, and hence we get *Avraham Eivril*. See also *Eiver*. Care must be taken not to confuse the diminutive *Avril* from *Avraham*; nor the diminutive *Evril* from *Efraiyim*. See also footnote 38. An added caution is to bear in mind that in Yiddish the א and the ע are sometimes capriciously interchanged.

Barukh (Benedict)[18] — בּרוך (בּענדעט)

Biblical. Yirmiyahu, 32:12.
"Blessed one." Scribe of the Prophet Yirmiyahu.

Borukh	בֵּענדט
Bendet[19, 20]	בֵּענדִיט[20, 19]
Bendet'l	בֵּענדֵעט[20, 19]
Bendit[20]	בֵּענדֵעטל

18. The Jewish family name *Benedikt* is derived from the Latin translation of *Barukh*.
19. The combined names *Barukh Bendet* is still in vogue.

20. The family name *Bennet* is derived from this form, the *d* having been elided. Other forms are *Baneth* (and even *Bineth*), *Paneth*, etc. The *b* and *p* are both labials and hence interchangeable.

Bentziyon (Benzion) — בנציון[21] בן ציון[21]

Hebrew. Non-biblical.
"Son of Zion." Revealing a longing for Yerushalayyim and the Holy Land of Yisrael.

Bentzion	בֵּענצל
Bentze	בֵּענטשׁע
Bentche	בֵּנצֶ׳ע
Bentzel	בֵּענצעל
Bentzil	בֵּענצִיל
Benchel	בֵּענטשׁעל
Benchil	בֵּענטשִׁיל

21. Can be written as one word or as two words, but only in Hebrew. In English it is normally written as one word.

Berekhyah — ברכיה

Biblical. Zekharyah, 1:7.
"Blessed of the Lord." Father of the Prophet Zekharyah.

Birakh	בֵּירֶך[22]
Birekh	
Beirakh	
Beirekh	
Beirikh	

22. See footnote 8.

Betzaleil — בצלאל

Biblical. Shemot.
"In the shade of the Lord." The biblical Betzalel was endowed with super artistic talents by the Almighty. Therewith he built the Sanctuary in the desert with all its artistic trappings, including the Golden Menorah. (Shemot 31:2-5)

Betzalel	צַאלל[23]
Tzalel	צַאלֶע
Zalel	צַאלְקֶע

Tzale[23]	צַאלְקַא
Zale	זַאלְקֶע
Tzalke	זַאלְקַא
Zalke[23a]	
Tzalka	
Zalka[23a]	

23. As explained in footnote 8, Jews avoided the use of God's name. Hence the suffix *el* was either shortened to *'l*, or elided to *e*.
23a. It is possible that the family names *Zalkin*, *Zalkind*, *Zelkin* and *Zelkind* are derived from this form.

Binyamin (Benjamin) בנימין

Biblical. Bereishit, 35:18.
Raḥel the Matriarch died in giving birth to this son. Her dying words were to name him Ben Oni, Son of my Sorrow. Yakov, the boy's father, immediately rejected this negative name and called him Binyamin. The simple meaning is "Son of the Right" (in contrast to the left, and inferring strength). But Rashi explains that it can also refer to the fact that Binyamin was the last son born to Yakov, and it thus can mean "Son of my Days", inferring that Binyamin was born in Yakov's old age. Father of the Tribe carrying his name.

Benyamin	בֵּיינִישׁ [24] [24a]
Benyomin	בֵּיינוּשׁ [24]
Beinush[24, 24a]	בֵּיינִיס
Beinish	בִּינִיס
Beinis[24]	
Binis	

24. שׁ and ס are both dentals and hence interchangeable.
24a. See footnote 1c.

Bunim (Bonim, Bon Nom)[25] בּוּנִים (בּאנִים שֹׁם טוב)[25]

Contraction of two French words.
"Good name." A translation of the Hebrew male name Shem Tov.

Bunim	בּוּנִים
Bunem	בּוּנֶעם
Bonim	בָּאנִים
Bonem	בָּאנֶעם
Binim	בִּינָים

Binem בִּינֶעם

25. Very often combined with the name *Simḥah* (*Simḥah Bunim*). Reason unknown. Some authorities claim that the name derives from the French *bon homme* (a good man). It is this author's contention that the name *Shem Tov* was very popular in pre-expulsion Spain; and this opinion is based on the dozens of Rabbis of pre-expulsion Spain who carried the Hebrew name *Shem Tov*. During the emigration to France, the name was translated to French. During the following centuries of wandering from country to country the two words *Bon Nom* became contracted to one word. Finally, the pronunciation was influenced by local phonetics. See also footnote 32 for the contraction of two names to form a new one.

I have yet to discover at any time in history, a Jew with the Hebrew name *Ish Tov*—a Good Man. A Yiddish name *Gutman* did eventually evolve independently. *Gutmann* (*Gutman*) also became a family name (and in English, *Goodman*).

Bueno (Spanish: good) was a popular name amongst Jews of the Iberian Peninsula.* It is this name that eventually became the Yiddish (read German) *Gutman*. The *Gut* meaning *good*, and the *man*, either the Old German diminutive suffix (see footnote 36), or simply the word for a *man*—meaning a *good man*. See also footnote 147a. For the female equivalent, see *Buna*.

* It is derived from the Hebrew name, *Toviyah (Tuviah)*.

Dani'eil (Daniel) דניאל

Biblical. Dani'eil, 1:6-7.
"Judged of the Lord." The Prophet of "The End of Days." He lived and preached in Babylon. He authored the Book of Dani'eil.

Dan'l[26] דַאנל[26]
Denel דֶענל
Dan[27] דַן[27]
Dani דַאני

26. See footnote 8.
27. *Dan* was an independent name even before the name Daniel. One of the sons of the Patriarch *Yakov (Jacob)* was named *Dan*, and hence the progenitor of the Tribe carrying his name.

David דוד

Biblical, Ruth, 4:13–21.
"A friend." The Royal House of David from whom the Messiah shall descend through the male line. Composer of most of the Books of Tehilim (Psalms).

Dovid	דָוִדל
Dovid'l	דָוִידקַא
Dovidka	דָוִידקֶע
Dovidke	דֶעווֶעל[28]
Devel[28]	דֶעווִיל
Devvil	טֶעווֶעל[29, 30]
Tevel[29, 30]	טֶעבֶעל[30]
Tevil	טֶעווִיל
Tevele[30]	טֶעבִיל
	טֶעווֶעלֶע[30]
	טֶעבֶעלֶע

28. This form was evolved by the elision of the second ד and the adding of the Germanic diminutive *el*—*Davel* became *Devel*.
29. ד and ט are both dentals and hence interchangeable.
30. The *v*-sounding consonant can be expressed with either the וו of Yiddish or the ב (Ashkenazi, pronunciation *veis*). This form *Tevel* in writing is not to be confused with the Yiddish diminutive *Tevia-Tevel* of *Tuviah*, nor with the female names *Teibel* and *Teibil*. See footnote 394.

Dov (Dov Ber)[31] — דוב (דוב בער)[31]

Hebrew. Non-biblical.
"A bear." One of the male animal names. In German, hence in Yiddish, *Ber*.

Dover[32]	דוֹבֶער[32]
Duber[32]	דוּבֶער[32]
Ber	בֶער
Bere	בֶערֶע
Berel	בֶערֶעל
Berele	בֶערֶעלֶע
Berelein	בֶערֶעלֵיין
Berlein	בֶערלֵיין
Berelin	בֶערֶעלִין
Berlin[33]	בֶערלִין[33]
Berke	בֶערקֶע
Berko[34]	בֶערקַא[34]
Berek	בֶערֶעק
Berik	בֶערִיק
Berish[34a]	בֶערִיש[34a]
Berush	בֶערוּש

Berman[35,36]	בֶּערמַאן[36, 35]
	בֶּערמַן

31. The Hebrew and Yiddish translation are often used together.
32. *Dov* and *Ber* share the same letters at the end of Do*v* and the beginning of *B*er. Phonetically it was inevitable that they should contract together to make one name. For another example, see *Bunim*.
33. *Berlin* became a popular family name and has no connection with the German capital. See footnote 135.
34. From *Berko* there developed amongst Slavic-speaking Jews, the family name *Berkowitz* and its variant spellings.

34a. See footnote 1c.

35. Also a popular family name.
36. *Mann* is another German diminutive suffix. When referring to one in the accusative case, *Mann* is attached to the name.

Efrayim (Fishel)[37] — אפרים (אפרים פישעל)[37]

Biblical. Bereishit, 41:52.
"Fruitful." From the root "Peri." The name is in the plural form. Yoseif's second son who, like his older brother Menashe, was born in Egypt. Yoseif therefore called this son Efrayim because, "God has caused me to be fruitful in the land of my misery." Father of the half-tribe carrying his name.

Efraiyim	אֶפְרָאם
Efrom	עֶפְרָאם
Efroimke	אֶפְרוֹימְקֶע
Efroimka	אֶפְרוֹימְקַא
Efroike	עֶפְרוֹימְקֶע
Efroika	עֶפְרוֹימְקֶע
Efroimel	עֶפְרוֹימְקַא
Froim	אֶפְרוֹימְעל
Froimke	עֶפְרוֹימְעל
Froimka	אֶפְרוֹיקַא
Froimel	עֶפְרוֹיקֶע
Evril[38]	עֶפְרוֹיקַא
Fish[39]	פרוֹיקֶע
Feish	פרוֹיקַא
Fishel[39]	פרוֹים
Fishil	פרוֹימְקֶע
Feishel	פרוֹימְקַא
Feishil	פרוֹימְעל
Vish'l[39a]	עֶבְרִיל[38]

Veish'l	פִּישֶׁעל[39]
	פִּישְׁל
	פִּישׁ[39]
	פֵּייש
	פֵּיישֶׁעל
	פֵּיישֶׁיל[39a]
	וִישְׁל
	וֵויישל

37. *Efraim* is often accompanied by *Fishel*. Patriarch *Yakov* blessed his grandson *Efraiyim* (son of *Yosef*) to multiply like the *fish* of the sea.
38. פ and ב are labio-dentals and hence interchangeable. See also footnote 17.
39. Both these forms became family names.
39a. See footnote 38.

Eiliyahu (Elijah) אליהו

Biblical. Melakhim I, 17:1.
"My God is Lord." Prophet of God, and the one who shall appear before the appearance of the Messiah to herald his coming. Tradition tells us that Eiliyahu shall go up on Mount Tziyon and blow on the Great Shofar. Tradition has it that Eiliyahu the Prophet attends the *brit milah* (circumcision) of every Jewish boy. He was one of those who never died. He went up into Heaven in a flaming chariot. He is the patron of all righteous people who are in trouble and appears disguised in many ways when helping them. Only the greatest piety can reward one with actually seeing Eiliyahu the Prophet when he is present at some event. The Talmud tells us that one of the Sages was visiting the marketplace when he suddenly saw Eiliyahu amongst the people. No one but this righteous Sage saw him. He greeted the Prophet and asked him who of all those present was sure to inherit the World to Come. Eiliyahu pointed to one man who was causing laughter amongst a group of people. The sage was a little taken aback. The Prophet then explained that the man making others happy and full of joy was really righteous in what he was doing. He made others happy and hence was certainly worthy to have a portion in the World to Come.

Eliyahu	עֶלְיַא[40]
Eliyohu	עֶלְיַה
Elya[40]	עֶליע
Elye	אֱלִי[41]
Eli[41]	עֶלִי[41]

Elik	אליק
Elinke	אלינקע
Elinka	אלינקא

40. The reason given in footnote 45 is impossible to apply to this name as it is a combination of two names of God. But in its written form some did change the א to the Yiddish ע. Even in speech the second syllable of the name was dropped because it, too, is a short name of God.
41. Notwithstanding what was mentioned in the previous footnote, that a shortened diminutive form of this name is, for the reasons stated above, written with an ע, it is not to be confused with the independent name *Eli* (written with an *ayyim* and) which was carried by the Prophet *Eli* who is written about in Shmuel I (Samuel I).

    This is another example of *reducio ad identicum.*

Eiver (Eber) עבר

Biblical. Bereishit, 10:21-22.
"To go over." Root of the word Ivri (a Hebrew). Note the structure of the non-Hebrew word "over" which in Hebrew would imply went or came over. The Hebrew for transgression is aveirah from the same root Ivri, "to go over from good to bad" (to pass over the right conduct).

Eivril[42]	עבריל[42]
Eiverman[43]	עברמן[43]

42. See footnote 17. See also footnote 38.
43. See footnote 36.

Elazar[44] (Lazarus) אלעזר[44]

Biblical. Shemot, 6:23.
"God has helped." Son of Aharon the High Priest.

Elozor	לאזאר[45]
Elozer	לאזער
Lozor[45]	לאזיר
Lozer	לוזר
Lozir	לוזער
	לוזיר

44. Often confused with *Eliezer*. They have since old been two distinct names, notwithstanding that they are etymologically identical.
45. Just as God's name as a suffix was avoided in daily speech, so was it

avoided with a prefix of a personal name. See footnote 5. We see in this form that the diminutive structure has elided the Hebrew א completely, concealing its theonymic origin.

Elḥanan — אלחנן

Biblical. Shmueil II, 23:24. Chronicles I, 11:26.
"God has graced." One of King David's better warriors.

Elḥonon	חָנָן[46]
Ḥanan[46]	חָאנִי
Ḥonon	חָאנֶע
Ḥoni	חָאנַא
Ḥone	
Ḥona	

46. See footnote 45. See also *Yoḥanan* and footnote 193.

Eliezer[47] — אליעזר[47]

Biblical. Bereishit, 15:2.
"My God helps." Servant of Avraham. He hailed from Damascus and was one of the Righteous Proselytes influenced by Avraham to forsake idolatry and to recognize and worship the One True God. Creator of all.

Leizer[48]	לֵייזֶר[48]
Leizir	לֵייזֶער
Leizerel	לֵייזִיר
Leizerke	לֵייזֶערֶעל
	לֵייזֶערְקֶע

47. See footnote 44.
48. See footnote 45.

Elimelekh (Elimelech) — אלימלך

Biblical. Ruth, 1:2.
"My God is king." Husband of Naomi, and first father-in-law of Ruth, progenitoress of King David.

Melekh[49, 50]	מֶלֶךְ[50, 49]
Melikh	מֶלִיךְ
Meilekh	מֶלֶעךְ
Meilikh	מֵיילֶעךְ
	מֵיילִיךְ

49. In all these diminutive forms the first syllable, the Lord's name, was elided. See footnotes 8 and 45.
50. This diminutive form has, in some cases, become an independent name.

Elyakim אליקים

Biblical. Melakhim II, 18:18.
"God will set up"—"Establish." An officer at the royal court of King Ḥizkiyahu.

Elyokim[51]	אֱלְיָקִים[51]
Elyakum[51, 52]	אֱלְיַקוּם[51, 52]
Elyokum	אֱלְיָקוּם
Yokim	יָקִים
Yokum	יָקוּם
Yoki	יוֹקִי

51. The Biblical spelling is Elyak*i*m with a י (*i*), but there developed a form with the spelling Elyak*u*m with a ו (*u*), also. The meaning remains the same.
52. See also *Gottschalk* and footnote 62.

Gedalyah (Gedaliah) גדליה

Biblical. Tzefanyah, 1:1. Melakhim II, 25:22, 25.
"Greatness of God"—"God is great." Paternal grandfather of Tzefanyah the Prophet.

Godul[53, 54]	גְדַלִיה[53]
Godel	גָדוּל[54, 53]
Godil	גָדֶעל
Godol	גָדִיל
	גָאדֶעל
	גָאדִיל
	גָאדָאל

53. See footnote 8.
54. There is a possibility that this name form is a diminutive of the name *Gad (God-el)* as expressed in the Ashkenazi pronunciation.

Gotthelf[54a] עזריאל

Biblical. Chronicles I, 27:19.
Hebrew: "My help is God"—German: "God's help." One of the heads of the father's of the half-tribe of Menasheh who was taken into

exile by the kings of Assyria.

Gotthelf[55]	עֲזְרִיל[56]
Azriel[57]	גוֹטְהֶעלף[55]
Ezriel[57]	גוֹטְהִילף
Esriel	

54a. *Gotthelf* and its reversed form *Helfgott* are also family names.

55. This German-Jewish name is a simple translation of the Hebrew. It also became a family name. It is a variation of *Eliezer* and *Elazar* (*Elozor*).

56. See footnote 8.

57. Many Jews with the name *Yisrael (Israel)* preferred using this name in daily contact with Gentiles and officialdom.

Gottlieb ידידיה

Biblical. Shmuel II, 12:24–25.
Hebrew: "Friend of God"—German: "Love of God." Natan the Prophet called Shlomoh Yedidyah when he was born to King David.

Gottlieb[58]	גָאטְלִיב[58]
Yedidyah	גוֹטְלִיב
Yedidiah	יְדִידִי[59]
Didya[59]	דִידְיַא
Didye	דִידְיֶע

58. A popular Jewish family name. See footnote 83. *Leibgott* in the reverse also became a family name.

59. See footnote 8.

Gottschalk[60] גוֹטשׁאלק[60]

Old German.
Schalk—"Unfaithful to;" Gott—"God." With theological implications.
See footnote 64.

Gottschalk[61]	גאטשַׁאלק[61]
Gotsh'l	גוֹטְשׁל
Gotsch	גוֹטשׁ
Goetz[61, 61a]	גוֹץ[61]
Getz[61, 62]	גֶעץ[62, 61]
Getzel[62]	גֶעצֶעל[62]

60. A theonymic name form. I have not ascertained the true meaning of its combination form. See footnote 62.

61. These have become family names.

61a. *Götz (Goetz)* is also the diminutive form of the German personal name *Gottfried* (at peace with God). This is a phonetic coincidence.

62. Mostly used in combination with the Hebrew name *Elyakim* (God will establish). The combination may be symbolic implying that, although the Jewish People were at times *unfaithful to God*, He would yet establish them as an independent people in their own land as had been prophesied by the Prophets. But why any Jew would want to adopt such a negative name still remains a riddle.

In Old German, "*Schalk*" means an unfaithful servant.

Ḥanokh[63, 64] (Enoch) — חֲנוֹךְ[64, 63]

Biblical. Bereishit, 5:18,21,24.
"Dedicated"—"Educated and raised correctly." Seventh generation from Adam. Son of Yered and father of Metushelah, the oldest human that ever lived—969 years. Ḥanokh was the great-grandfather of Noaḥ. The Torah records that he did not die, but was taken alive to God on account of righteousness.

Henikh	הֶענֶאךְ
Heinikh	הֶענִיךְ
Henel	הֵיינִיךְ
Henli	הֶענֶעל
Hendl[65]	הֶענְלִי
Hendel[65]	הֶענְדְל[65]
Hendil[65]	הֶענְדֶעל[65]
Enikh[63]	הֶענְדִיל[65]
Einikh	עֶנִיךְ[63]
	אֵיינִיךְ

63. The Hebrew letter ח is in the velar group. The phonetic influences of many European countries either softened this letter to a simple Anglo-Saxon *h*, or hardened it to the Germanic glottal *ch* as in the Scottish *Loch*, and in some cases it was even elided.

64. Also see *Zundel*.

65. Such are the vicissitudes of phonetics that these forms are also diminutives of the female name *Hinde*. See also footnote 9. Also developed into a family name.

Another family name derivative is *Hendelman* or *Handelman* (see footnote 36), which coincidently means a man dealing in business.

Ḥayyim חיים

Hebrew. Non-biblical.
"Life"— "Living"— "Alive."

Ḥai
Ḥayyiman
Heiman[66]
Heyman[66]
Ḥayyimel
Ḥayyimka
Ḥayyimke
Ḥaikel[66a]
Ḥeikel[66a]
Vital[67]
Vidal[67]
Feitel[68]
Veis[67]
Feis[67]
Feist[67]

חַי
חַיימַאן
הֵיימַאן[66]
חַיימֶעל
חַיימְקַא
חַיימַקֶע
חַייקֶעל[66a]
וִויטַאל[67]
וִוידַאל[67]
פֵייטֶעל[68]
וֵייס[67]
פֵייס[67]
פֵייסט[67]

66. *Heiman* and *Heyman* became Jewish family names.
66a. Both these forms developed into family names.
67. The ט and the ד both belong to the dental group and are hence interchangeable. *Vital* and *Vidal* are Italian translations of *Ḥayyim*. They became family names; especially among Sefardi Jews. *Vie*, *Vives*, *Vif* and *Vifs* are various forms of the French for *Ḥayyim*. *V* and *f* are both labio-dentals and hence interchangeable. The erroneous assumption made by the late Prof. Gumpretz, which was discussed in footnote 142, was due also to his overlooking the fact that *two* names are involved. *Feivush* and *Feis* developed independently, and the learned professor presumed them to be one and the same origin. The form *Feist* with the added *t* is a coloquial phonetic abberation.
68. A Yiddish extension of *Vital*. The ו and the פ both belong to the labio-dental group, as mentioned in the previous footnote, and are hence interchangeable. The family names *Faitelovitch* or *Faitlovitch* derive from this form. The German Jewish family name *Veit* may be a shortened derivation of *Feitel*. See footnote 38.

Ḥizkiyahu חזקיהו

Biblical. Melakhim II, 18:1.
"Strengthened by the Lord"—"My strength is the Lord." King of Yehudah.

Ḥizkiyohu
Hiz[69] — הִיז[69]
Hess[70, 71] — הֶעס[71, 70]

69. See footnote 63.
70. ז and ס are both dentals and hence interchangeable.
71. A Jewish family name *Hess*, and also *Hass*, has developed in German speaking countries.

Immanu'eil — עמנואל

Biblical. Yeshaiyahu 7:14
"God is with us." Son of the Prophet Yeshaiyahu.

Emanuel — מַנוּאֶל
Manuel — מֶענִי[72]
Meni[72] — מָאנִי
Moni — מָאנְיֶע
Monye — מַאנְיַא
Monya — מָאנְיַא[73]
Manya[73] — מַאנֶעל
Monel — מָאנוֹיל
Monoil

72. See footnote 8.
73. Not to be confused with the female name *Manya*. This is just another example of phonetical coincidence.

Kalonymus — קלונימוס

Old Greek.
Kalon—"beautiful;" Nymus—"name." Possibly another attempt at translating the Hebrew name Shem Tov. The use of this name by Jews is from the Second Temple period.

Kalman[74] — קַלְמַן[74]
Kalmenka[75] — קַלְמֶנְקַא[75]
Kalmenke[75] — קַלְמַנְקֶע[75]

74. Often used together after the original name form—*Kalonymus*.
75. A branch of the ancient family *Yoffe* (*Yaffe*, *Joffe*, *Jaffe*, etc.) which means beautiful, had a progenitor called *Kalman* (beautiful name) *Yoffe*. They changed their name to *Yoffe-Kalmenkes* (beautiful, beautiful name). *Kalminkes*, alone, is also a family name.

Kuni[76] — קוּנִי[76]

Old Spanish.
"Childish"—"Babyish." Amongst others, one large family of Spanish-Jewish exiles, carrying the family name Kuni made their way to Salonika, Greece, via Sicily. We have no way of knowing why such a family name was adopted. It is interesting to note that the name has persisted amongst Ashkenazi Jews as a personal name, both male and female.

Kooni	קוּנֵע[77a]
Kuna[77, 77a]	קוּנַא[77a, 77]
Kune[77a]	קוּנְיֵע
Kunya	קוּנְיַא
Kunye	

76. See footnote 78.
77. See also the female name *Kuna*.
77a. The family name *Kunin* derived from these forms.

Lemu'eil[78] — לְמוּאֵל[78]

Biblical. Proverbs, 31:2-9.
Lemu/Lemo plus Eil. A contraction of both words. "Belonging to God." The opening passage of Proverbs, 31:1 can be read in two ways, with two results. If the comma is placed after the word melekh (king), then it refers to King Shlomoh, and it then means that he is counselling with his mother's advice, and he was also called Lemueil (belonging to God), as one dedicating his life to serving God. Other authorities claim that the comma should be after the next word Massa, and that the counsel is the words of the mother of Lemueil, King of Massa. The passage would then be a general advice to all kings, with Lemueil used as the negative example of a foolish king.

Lemuel	לֶעמֶע
Lemoel	לֶעמֶעל[79]
Leme	לֶעמְלַא
Lemel[79]	לֶעמְלֶע
Lemla	לֶעמְקֶע
Lemle	לֶעמְקִי
Lemke	לֶעמְקֶען
Lemki	לֶעמְקִין
Lemken	לֶעמְלֵיין
Lemkin	לֶעמְלִין

Lemlein	לַאם[80]
Lemlin	לַאמְלִין
Lam[80]	לִימַא
Lamlin	לֵיימַא
Lima	לִימַאן
Leima	לֵיימַאן[81]
Liman	לֶעמְעכֶעל[82]
Leiman[81]	לֶעמְעכִיל
Lemekhel[82]	
Lemekhil	

78. A biblical non-Jewish foolish king (see Proverbs 31:2-9). He was apparently unwise in his drinking habits and immature in his choice of women. Even in contemporary times we often call an immature or naive person a *Kuni Lemel*. *Kuni* is Old Spanish for baby or baby-like. In modern Spanish, it means a cradle. During the Expulsion, Spanish Jews carrying the family name *Kuni* migrated to Salonika via Sicily.
79. The name *Asher* also is often combined with *Lemel*. The reason is unclear.
80. The family name *Lamm* and *Lam* developed from this form.
81. Also developed into a family name.
82. The basic name, in this case, is the diminutive *Leme*. The *Khel* is a double diminutive suffix. It has no connection with *Lemekh*, the father of *Noaḥ*, but is used in Yiddish to denote childish or naive.

Lieber[83] — ליבער[83]

German.
"Lovable." A name of endearment. Used in Yiddish.

Liber[83]	לִיבֶּר
Liber'l[84]	לִיבֶּרְעל
Liberman[83]	לִיבֶּערְל[84]
Lieberman[83]	לִיבֶּערמַאן[83]
Liebman[83]	לִיבֶּערמַן
Lippa[85]	לִיבְמַאן[83]
Lippe	לִיפַּא[85]
Lipman[83]	לִיפֶּע
Lippman[83]	לִיפְּמַאן[83]
Lippmann[83]	לִיפְקַא[86]
Lipka[86]	לִיפְקֶע[86]
Lipke[86]	

83. These have developed into family names.*
84. See footnote 65, and diminutive forms of female name *Lieba*.
85. *B* and *p* are both labials and hence interchangeable. The word derives

from the Sanskrit *Luba*, meaning "love." It came through the Indo-European language group into the Old German *Lüber*, and then into *Leiber*. In Russian, it is still *Luba*. (Also a girl's name—into Yiddish *Lieba*. See entry *Lieba* in female index.) The word survived in English as *Love*.

86. The family names *Lipkin* and *Lipkes* derive from these forms. The family name *Lipsky*, however, is a place name derivative. It derives from the city of *Lipsk* which lies close to Kovno.

* It is possible that the name *Lieber* is a breakaway from the full name *Gottlieb* and became detached due to the Jewish sensitivity of uttering God's name in vain. See *Gottlieb* and also footnote 8.

Mei'ir — מאיר

Hebrew. Non-biblical.
"To give light"—"To enlighten." The Mishnaic Sage Rabbi Mei'ir was instructed by his teacher Rabbi Akivah to gather all the oral teachings of the Torah from all the Sages of Yisrael. The idea was to preserve the oral Torah from being forgotten by the Jewish People. This occurred during the time of the Roman conquest of the Holy Land when the teaching of the Torah was punishable by death. Rabbi Akivah was eventually martyred by the Romans for teaching Torah, but Rabbi Mei'ir succeeded in his task. Whenever a law is stated in the Mishnah without the name of the rabbinic source behind it, it is always accredited to Rabbi Mei'ir. Beruryah, the wife of Rabbi Mei'ir, was a famous personality in her own right. She was the only woman to have had a law quoted in her name in the Talmud.

Meir	מֵאִירֶעל
Mei'irel	מֵאִירִיל
Mei'iril	מֵאִירְקֶע
Mei'irke	מַהַרַ"ם[87]
Maharam[87]	מַארַאם[87]
Maram[87]	מַארֶעם[87]
Marem[87]	מַארִים[87]
Marim[87]	מַארוֹם[87]
Marum[87]	מֵיירם[87]
Meiram[87]	מֵיירַאם[87]
Mairem[87]	מֵיירֶעם[87]

87. This is an acronym of the name of the martyred Rabbinic scholar *Moreinu Harav Meir* of Rottenburg (c.1215–1293). Possibly the only acronym to have been diminutised into a personal name. He was so beloved of his students, that many of them named a son after him even using his

acronym. Obviously his descendants also named their sons in the same fashion. It would be correct to assume that any family with a tradition of this personal acronymic male name descends from either the martyred Rabbi Meir of Rottenburg or from a disciple of his.

Menaḥeim מנחם

Biblical. Melakhim II, 15:14.
"Comforter"—"To comfort." Sixteeth king of Yisrael.

Menaḥem	מאן[88]
Mann[88]	מן
Mannele	מנלי
Mannkhen[89]	מנעלע
Menka	מנכען[89]
Menke	מנקה
Mendel[90]	מענקה
Mendil	מענדעל[90]
Mendl	מענדיל
Munczia	מונציא
Menni	מעני
Menkhin	מענכין

88. This form developed into a family name.
89. Not to be confused with Mannheim, the name of a German town.
90. The dynamics of certain Old German phonetics can cause a name ending in *n* to extend its diminutive suffix into *del*, *dil*, or *dl*. Notwithstanding that the abbreviated form is *Mann*, *Men*-del sticks to the original first vowel *e* because it would end up otherwise as *Mandel* which in German (read Yiddish) means an almond, and this would be phonetically untenable.

The family name Mendelbaum presumably derives from the name M*a*ndelbaum, the *a* having been replaced with the *e* because of the common use of Men-del as a personal name.

Menaḥem Mendel is a common combination.

In passing, let me demonstrate one of the marvels of linguistics and phonetics. As is known, English is an Anglo-Saxon language which means that it is based on the Germanic tongue (but not exclusively). *Mandel* in German is an "almond." In this case of word borrowing the *el* of Mand*el* was switched to the beginning of the word in English and ended up as *al*mond.

Menashe מְנַשֶּׁה

Biblical. Bereishit, 41:50-51.
"To make forget." In the original naming of Menasheh, his father Yoseif expressed the sentiment that with the birth of the child, his troubles were made to be forgotten. He was the first born of Yoseif and Asnat. Father of the half-tribe carrying his name.

Manish	מַאנִישׁ
Monish	מָאנִישׁ
Monash[91]	מָאנַאשׁ[91]
Mannes[92, 93]	מַאנֶעס[93, 92]
Mannis	מַאנִיס
Monnis	מוֹנִיס

91. At least one Jewish family adopted this form of the diminutive as a family name, the celebrated General Sir John *Monash* of Melbourne, Australia. His mother was a sister of the more famous Jewish historian, Heinrich Graetz.
92. This diminutive form *Mannes* also became a family name.
93. ס and שׁ are both dentals and hence interchangeable.

Meshulam[94] מְשׁוּלָם[94]

Biblical. Melakhim II, 22:3.
"Paid for"—"Bought for money"—"Compensated for." The paternal grandfather of Shafan, the scribe of Yoshiyah, King of Yehudah.

Shulam	שׁוּלַם
Shil'm	שִׁילְם
	שִׁילִים
Shalom[95]	
Sholom	שָׁלוֹם[95]
Shulman[96, 97]	שׁוּלְמַאן[97, 96]
	שׁוּלְמַן

94. A biblical name. Probably expressing the idea that the Lord had given the parents a child, either after a long period of childlessness, or as a reward for righteous living.
95. See also *Shalom (Sholom)* which became an independent name over 4,000 years ago.
96. See footnote 36.
97. The popular family name *Shulman* derives from this form. It does not derive from the Yiddish word *shule*—synagogue.

Mikha'eil מיכאל

Biblical. Dani'eil, 12:1.
"Who is like God?" (Who can be compared to God?) Name of the second Angel, after Gavri'eil, who appeared to Dani'eil in his Prophetic vision, to reassure him with good counsel and the protection of the Jewish People.

Mikhael	מִיכַל[98]
Mikhoel	מִיכְלִין[99]
Mikhal[98]	אִיכְל מִיכְל[100]
Mikhlin[99]	
Ikhal Mikhal[100]	

98. By eliding the א from the name, one avoided the use of God's name. See also footnote 8.
99. This form became a family name. Possibly also from the female name *Miklah*.
100. An uncommon form derived from phonetic playfulness. See also *Yeḥi'eil*, which together with *Mikhal* is a popular combination of names. This rare form *Ikhal Mikhal* became so entrenched that it was used even for one whose name was *Mikhal* only.

Mordekhai[100a] (Mordecai) מרדכי

Biblical. Esteir, 2:5.
Notwithstanding that the name could be a derivative of the name of the Persian god, Merodakh, the Talmudic Sages, in the Tractate Hulin, 139b, state that the name is Aramaic and composed of two words—Mor Dekhi—which means "bitter freedom." Mordekhai was of the Tribe of Binyamin. He authored the Megillat Esteir, read on Purim.

Mordel	מוֹרְדל
Mordush[100b]	מוֹרְדוּשׁ[100b]
Motta[101]	מוֹטַא[101]
Motte	מוֹטֶע
Motka	מוֹטְקַא
Motke	מוֹטְקֶע
Moddel	מוֹדל
Mottel	מוֹדֶעל
Morkl[102]	מוֹטל
Morkel	מוֹטֶעל
Morkil	מָארְקל[102]
	מָארְקִיל

	מָארקֶעל
	מָרקְל
	מָרקִיל
	מָרקֶעל

100a. A family name *Mordech* derived from the basic name.
100b. See footnote 7c.
101. See footnote 29.
102. In these cases the ד has been elided and then the diminutive suffix was added.

Moshe (Moses) משה

Biblical. Shemot, 2:1.
"To withdraw"—"To save from harm." Leader of the Jewish People who, with the help of the Almighty, led his people out of the Egyptian bondage, through the desert, and up to the Holy Land. Divinely inspired, he wrote the Five Books carrying his name.

Moshka[103]	מָאשְׁקַא[103]
Moshke	מָאשְׁקַה
Moishe	מָאשְׁקֶע
Meisha[104]	מוֹשְׁקַא
Meishe	מוֹשְׁקַה
Meishel[105]	מוֹשְׁקֶע
Meishil	מֵיישַׁא[104]
Meshel[106]	מֵיישֶׁע
Meshil	מֵיישֶׁעל[105]
	מֵיישִׁיל
	מֶעשֶׁעל[106]
	מֶעשִׁיל

103. The family name *Moscowitz* can also be geographic in origin—*Moshkowitz* or *Moscowitz*.
104. The *oi* sound in Lithuanian and White Russian Hebrew and Yiddish is pronounced as *ei*. (Distant as they were geographically and linguistically, many Yemenite Jews also pronounce the *oi* as *ei*.) See footnote 106.
105. All variations of the family name *Meisel*, *Meisels*, *Maisel*, *Maislish*, *Meizel*, *Maizel*, etc., derive from these forms.*
106. In an article entitled "Jews in Ancient China—A Historical Survey," the author, Pan Guangdan, writes on page 200 (in the journal *Social Sciences in China*) in reference to a people in China in the medieval period, that they were known as "Disciples of *Moses*." He further states, "For them, *Moses* was only one of the chief founders and was called *Meshe* by the

Jews according to the two inscriptions by Jin Zhong and Zuo Tang." Again on page 208, he writes, "... our orthodox master *Meshe (Moses)....*"

This is an amazing discovery. That the ancient Jews of China, whose origin is still an open question with all the scholars of this subject, pronounced their *oi* as *ei*, should certainly have led these experts to the conclusion that the "Chinese Jews" hailed from a Yemenite background. If, as they claim, these Jews came from India, then surely their Indian migratory springboard was preceded by a Yemenite origin. In this case, the phonetics could probably have helped in solving the mystery. Jews from Aden, a southern Yemenite port, are known to have migrated north to Egypt, southwest to eastern Africa, and also to the west coast of India.

* The name may be derived from the stonecutter's trade. *Meissel* in German means a chisel.

Naftali (Naphtali)[107] נפתלי

Biblical. Bereishit, 30:8.
Son of Yakov and Bilhah. Father of the Tribe carrying his name. There are a number of possible meanings of this name. It depends on how one extracts the root of the word. It can be from Petil, a "bond," here meaning a bond with God. It can also be from the root Nafal, "to fall (prostate) in prayer." Another root could be Naftul, "to wrestle with"—hand to hand combat.

Naftoli[108]	טאלי
Tolli	נטי
Natty	נפתלי הערץ[109]
Naftoli Hertz[109]	

107. In his classic commentary on the Torah, Rashi explains the meaning of the name (Genesis, 30:8) as being from the word *tefilah* (prayer) and translates as "my prayer was accepted."
108. The family names *Naftolis* and *Naftolin* derive from the Ashkenazi pronunciation of this name.
109. The tribal symbol of *Naftali* is the deer, and the name often combines with the Yiddish *hertz* (deer). Much is recorded in Jewish tradition about the swiftness of foot of the progenitor of this Tribe. Ironically, based on this tradition, the Israel Postal Service selected a running deer as their symbol of quick delivery.

Natan (Nathan) נתן

Biblical. Shmuel II, 12:1, 5:14.
"He (God) gave." A Prophet of God in the times of King David and King Shlomoh. Also, King David had a son called Natan.

Nosson	נָתָן נָאטַא[110]
Nosson Notta[110]	נָתָן נָאטֶע[110]
Nosson Notte[110]	נָאשֶׁעל[111]
Nossel[111]	נָאטַא
Notta	נָאטֶע
Notte	נָאטֶעל
Nottel	נָאטֶעלֶע
Nottele	נָאטְקַא[112]
Notka[112]	נָאטְקֶע[112]
Notke[112]	נָאטִינְקַא
Notinka	נָאטִינְקֶע
Notinke	

110. With Hebrew names, the diminutive form is often used together with the original Hebrew, (i.e. *Menaḥem Mendel, Shmuel Shmelke*).
111. From this form there derived the family name *Nossell.*
112. The family name *Notkin* and *Natkin* derive from the diminutive forms.

Netaneil (Nathaniel) נתנאל

Biblical. Bamidbar, 1:8.
"God has given." A chief of the Tribe of Yisakhar.

Natanel	סַאנֶעל
Nasanel[113]	סַאנֶע[113]
Sanel	
Sanne[114]	

113. The Ashkenazi pronunciation of the original ת is *sav* (sov). The non-Yemenite Eastern Jews pronounce it as *tav*. To this writer's knowledge, only the Yemenite Jews pronounce the letter as *th* (*thav*). The English transliteration has maintained the original pronunciation.
114. See footnote 8.

Pinḥas[115] (Phineas) פנחס[115]

Biblical. Shemot, 6:25.
"Mouth of a snake." The name is usually broken into two

Hebrew words: *pi* (mouth), and *nahash* (snake). It is difficult to understand why parents would give such a name to their son. Notwithstanding that in proper names the Hebrew letters ס, שׂ, and שׁ are interchanged, the Hebrew word for snake is written with a שׁ, and the name Pinḥas is written with a ס.

It seems to me that another breakdown of the name is also possible. *Pin* (face) and *ḥas* (compassion). It makes more sense to call a child the one with the "compassionate face."

Pinḥas was the son of Elazar the son of Aharon the High Priest. Angered by the desecration of the name of God, he rose in the defense of the Almighty's honour and slew Zimri, a chief of the Tribe of Shimon who had brazenly brought a Midionite woman into the Jewish camp and had relations with her during a session of Torah that was being held by Moshe and all the chiefs of all the Tribes of Yisrael. The name is the symbol of one who defends the honour of God.

Pinna	פִּינָא
Pinne	פִּינֶע
Pinya	פִּינְיָא
Pinye	פִּינְיֶע
Pinnel	פִּינֶעל
Pinḥas'l	פִּינְחַסל

115. In this case, the ח became hardened and eventually developed into a *k*. From the form of the word thus developed, there evolved the family name *Pinkus* and *Pincus*, especially amongst Anglo-Saxon Jews.

Refa'eil (Raphael) רפאל

Biblical. Chronicles I, 26:7.
"The Lord has healed." One of the Jews who went up to the Holy Land from the Babylonian exile.

Rafael	פָּאל[116]
Fol[116]	פָּאלְע
Folle	פּוֹלְע
Folk[117]	פָּאלק[117]
Follik	פּוֹלק
Folka	פָּאלִיק
Folke	פָּאלְקָא
	פּוֹלְקָא
	פָּאלְקֶע
	פּוֹלְקֶע

116. The ר has been elided together with the suffix which is God's name. See also footnote 24.

117. More often written as *Falk*. There is much speculation amongst the authorities as to why the name *Falk* is used together with *Yehoshua* (*Joshua*)—it has no relation to this diminutive of *Rafael*. Phonetically, this Yiddish diminutive form, when written in Hebrew letters, could be read as *Pollak* (of Polish origin), but this would still not explain the riddle of the *Yehoshua Falk* combination. *Falk* is a common family name that may have derived from this form.

Shabtai (Shabetai) שבתי

Biblical. Ezra, 10:15.
"Born on Shabbat"—"Sabbatical." One of the head Levites of those that returned to the Holy Land from the Babylonian exile.

Shabsi	שַׁבְּתַאי
Shabsil	שַׁבְּתִיל
Shabsel	שַׁבְּתֶעל
Shabtil	שֶׁעבְּטִיל
Shabtel	שֶׁעבְּטֶעל
Shebtil	שֶׁעפְּסִיל[118]
Shebtel	שֶׁעפְּסֶעל
Shepsil[118]	שֶׁעפְּטִיל[119]
Shepsel	שֶׁעפְּטֶעל
Sheptil[119]	
Sheptel	

118. ב and פ are labials and hence interchangeable.

119. See footnotes 9 and 122.

Shakhna שכנא

Biblical. Ezra, 10:2, Neḥemiyah, 6:18, 12:3, Chronicles I, 3:21, 24:11, Chronicles II, 31:15.
"To dwell"—"To be a neighbour"—"In the presence of." Probably a shortened form (diminutive) of the full name Shekhanyah—"in the presence of God." Six biblical personalities carried this name.

Shakhne	שַׁכְנֶע
Shekhna	שֶׁכְנַא
Shekhne	שֶׁכְנֶע
Shalom Shakhna[120]	שָׁלוֹם שַׁכְנַא[120]
Sholom Shakhna	

120. This combination is very common and the reason therefore is to be found in the Babylonian Talmud, Tractate Shabbat, Folio 12a–12b. Differences of opinions arose amongst the Sages as to the wording of the greetings on visiting and departing from a sick person on the Shabbat. Only one Sage insisted on including the word Shalom in both greetings. His name was Rabbi *Shabna* the Jerusalemite. In his commentary, *Tosfot* says that his name could not have been *Shabna*, and that it was *Shakhna*. He points out that the biblical *Shabna* was an evil Jew who betrayed his people during the war with *Sancherib*. Hence the name was changed long ago to *Shakhna*.

By his insistence on the use of the word Shalom in greeting the sick on Shabbat, this Sage *Shakhna* created the basis for combining the two names *Shalom Shakhna*.

Shalom   שָׁלוֹם

Hebrew. Non-biblical.
"Peace"—"A man of peace." A tombstone inscription in the German colony, a suburb of Jerusalem, carries the names Shalom and Mattyah, her sons, Shlomtzion and Dostam. The name Shalom, here inscribed, refers to a woman. The grave and its tombstone antedates 1500 CE.

Sholom   שׁוֹלָם[121]
Shulom[121]

121. Not to be confused with the name *Meshulam*.

Sha'ul (Saul)   שָׁאסל

Biblical. Shmuel I, 9:1–2.
"Requested"—"Asked for"—"Borrowed."
First king of the Jewish People. Annointed by Shmuel the Prophet. It is recorded that he was a very tall man.

Sholikeh   שָׁאוֹלִיקֶע
Sha'oil   שָׁאוֹיל
Shoi'el[122]   שׁוֹיאַל[122]
Shoi'l[123]   שׁוֹיל[123]

122. The name means to ask (request), and grammatically the word should be written *Sho-El*. That would entail using God's name every time the name was spoken. The Bible itself already made the provision to forestall the Lord's name being taken in vain, and from its inception, the name was written as *Sha-ul*. Thus, the combination of the *e* and the *l* (God's name) was avoided from the outset. With all this foresight and

provision, the dynamics of phonetics still developed a diminutive form which arrived at what was desired to be avoided.

123. See footnote 24.

Shefatyah שְׁפַטְיָה

Biblical. Shmuel II, 3:4.
"God has judged." A son who was born in Ḥevron to King David and his wife Avital.

Sheptayah	שֶׁעפְּטֶעל[124] [125]
Sheptel[124] [125]	שֶׁעפְּטִיל
Sheptil	שֶׁעפְּטְל[126]
Shept'l[126]	

124. Not to be confused with the diminutive *Sheptel* which is derived from *Shabtai*.
125. See footnote 9.
126. See footnore 24.

Shimon (Simeon, Simon) שִׁמְעוֹן

Biblical. Bereishit, 29:33.
"Hear my Affliction." Son of Yakov and Lei'ah. Together with his brother Leivi, they took revenge on Shekhem for having outraged their sister Dinah. Father of the Tribe carrying his name.

Shimonel	שִׁימָאנֶעל
Shimonka	שִׁימָאנְקַא
Shimonke	שִׁימָנְקֶע
Sheima	שֵׁיימַא
Sheime	שֵׁיימַה
Zimmel[127, 128]	שֵׁיימֶע
Zimmil	זִימֶעל[128, 127]
Zimmul	זִימִיל
	זִימוּל

127. ש and ז are both dentals and hence interchangeable.
128. A family name derived from this form.

Shlomoh (Solomon) שְׁלֹמֹה

Biblical. Shmuel II, 5:14, Chronicles I, 22:9.
"Peaceful"—"Man of peace." Son of King David and his wife Batsheva. Third king of Yisra'eil. He ruled for 40 years. The Prophet Natan called him also Yedidyah. He built the first Holy Temple in Jerusalem. Author of Proverbs, Song of Songs and Kohelet.

Shloimah	שלוֹמְקַא
Shlomka	שלוֹמְקֶע
Shlomke	שלוֹמֶעל
Shlomel	שלוֹמל
Zalman[129]	זַלְמַן[129]
Zaman'l	זַלְמַנל
Zalmanka[130]	זַלְמַנְקַא[130]
Zalmanke	זַלְמַנְקֶע
Zelman	זֶעלְמַאן
Zelmen	זֶעלְמֶען
Zalmina	זַלְמִינַא
Zelmina	זֶעלְמִינַא
Shlomoh Zalman	שְׁלֹמֹה זַלְמַן

129. See footnote 13.
130. *Zelminkas* and *Zelminkes* are two variations of a family name derived from these forms.

Shlumi'eil שְׁלֻמִיאֵל

Biblical. Bamidbar, 1:6.
"At peace with God." Son of Tzurishadai and a chief of the Tribe of Shimon.

Shlumiel	שלֶעמִיעֶל[131]
Shlomiel	
Shlemiel[131]	

131. In Yiddish, it has become a popular name for a fool or incompetent.

[A clever wit wanted to describe the difference between a *Shlemiel* and a *Shlimazal*—German: *Shlim* (bad), Hebrew: *Mazal* (luck). He described it thus: The *Shlemiel* is the one that spills hot soup all over the *Shlimazal*.]

There is a masculine German slang word *schlamassel* which describes one who has gotten himself into a scrap, fix, mess or jam. See *Cassell's German/English, English/German Dictionary*, London, 1968. Notwithstanding that there is also a masculine German word *schlamm* which means "slime" or "mud," the above slang word *schlamassel* is a good example of a reverse borrowing—from Yiddish.

Shmaryahu שמריהו

Biblical. Chronicles I, 12:5.
"The Lord guards"—"The Lord watches over us." One of the warriors of the Tribe of Binyamin who presented themselves to David when he was still hiding from King Sha'ul in the city of Ziklag. David heard the news that King Sha'ul and his son Yehonatan had been slain, and he then went to claim the kingship.

Shmaryah[132]	שְׁמַרְיַה[132]
Shmer'l[133]	שְׁמֶערל[133]
Shmerel	שְׁמֶערֶעל
Shmeril	שְׁמֶערִיל
Shmerlin[134]	שְׁמֶערְלִין[134]
Shmerlein[135]	שְׁמֶערְלֵיין[135]

132. An elided form.
133. It would be interesting to discover the historical reasons why this diminutive form is used in reference to a fool or naive person.
134. The family name *Shmerling* derives from this form.
135. *Lein* is an Old German diminutive suffix that can phonetically also end up as *Lin*. It implies "dear little one," that is, *frau* in German is an adult woman, and frau*lein* is a young woman. See also Ber*lin*, Isser*lin*.

Shmu'eil (Samuel) שמואל

Biblical. Shmueil I, 1:20.
"The Lord has heard or harkened to." Prophet of God. Son of Elkanah the Levite and his wife Hannah. The Prophet's mother was barren, and she came from time to time to the sanctuary in Shiloh to pray to conceive a child. When the Lord harkened to her prayers and she conceived and bore a son, she called him Shmu'eil and dedicated him to a life of serving the Almighty. He wrote the two books carrying his name.

Shmuel	שְׁמוּלְקַא[136]
Shmulka[136]	שְׁמוּלְקֶע
Shmulke	שְׁמֶעלְקַא
Shmelka	שְׁמֶעלְקֶע
Shmelke	שְׁמוּלִיק[136]
Shmulik[136]	זַאנְוִויל[137]

Zanvil[137] — זַאנְבִיל
Zavil[137, 138] — זַאוִויל[137, 138]
Zavel[137, 138] — זַאבִיל[137, 138]
Mulka — זַאבְל[137, 138]
Mulke — מוּלְקָא
Mulik — מוּלְקֶע
מוּלִיק

136. The author seems to have detected a Polish diminutive variation, *ek* and *ik*; and a Russian diminutive variation, *ka* and *ke*.
137. See footnote 13. Also, מ and נ are both dentals and hence interchangeable. The Hebrew letter ו is both a vowel *u* (as in pull) and a consonant *v*.
138. The נ has been elided = *Shmuel—Shemul—Shemv'l—Zemvil—Zanvil—Zavil*.

As this form contains the letter *veit* ב, *beit* (בּ) which is one and the same letter in written Hebrew, it is possible that the family name *Zabel* is a derivative of this form.

Shnei'or[139] — שְׁנֵיאוֹר[139]

Hebrew. Non-biblical.
Contraction of two words: שְׁנֵי (two), and אוֹר (light). "Two lights." In his *Responsa*, Rabbi Shlomoh Luria (?1510–1574) relates the following: One of his forebearers had a son and he wanted to call him Mei'ir after his father but his wife, the child's mother, wanted to call her son Yair after her father. Both names have their roots in the Hebrew word אוֹר (light), and so the parents compromised and called the child Shnei'or (Two lights). (This is not to prove that this was the first time such a compromise was made; it is the earliest record of such.)

Shner — שְׁנֶער
Shnei'or Zalman[140] — שְׁנֵייעֶר
Shnei'ur Zalman — שְׁנֵיאוֹר זַלְמָן[140]
שְׁנֵיאוּר זַלְמָן

139. There is much controversy about the etymological origin of this name. Suffice to mention two theories: One opinion claims it is two Hebrew words *Shnei Or*—Two Lights. The other maintains it is a corruption of the Spanish *Señor*.
140. A popular combination of names. See also *Shlomoh Zalman*. Thousands of his followers named a son after the founder of the Lubavitcher Dynasty, Rabbi *Shnei'or Zalman* of Liadi (Mohilev gubernia, White Russia).

Shraga[141] Feivush[142] — שרגא[141] פייבוש[142]

Aramaic.
"Light"—"Lamp"—"Lantern."

Feivish — פייביש
Feivel — פייווש
Feivil — פייוויל
Feivul — פייבול
Veibush[142] — ווייבוש[142]
Veibish — ווייביש

141. *Shraga* is the Aramaic word for light, and as a name it is akin to the Hebrew *Uri* and *Mei'ir.* Some who wanted a Hebrew name, also, are know as *Uri Shraga Feivel*—Hebrew, Aramaic, and Greek.

142. *Phoebus* is Greek for "light." The distorted assumptions of the late *Yehiel* Gompretz (Tarbitz," 25th. year, 1956, page 345–346 (6)–(7), Magnes Press, Hebrew University, Jerusalem) to prove that this name is a corruption of the French work *vives* which means *ḥayyim* (life) in Hebrew is untenable. That the *f* and *v* are both labio-dentals and hence interchangeable is certainly correct, but Gompertz's unproven assumption is based on the argument that *Phoebus* was the Greek deity of light and no Jew would assume the name of a pagan deity.

He continues his argument by stating that medieval Jewry was ignorant of the fact that *Phoebus* was the name of a pagan deity, and hence used the name *Phoebus* in conjunction with *Uri* or *Shraga* because it meant light. He brings no arguments why the name *vives—ḥayyim—life* should be combined with *Shraga.* His last argument is in itself a contradiction of his earlier statement that the Jews of the time did not know the true meaning of the Greek *Phoebus.* He also overlooked the fact that the two great pious biblical personalities, *Mordecai* and *Esther*, possibly also carried the names of Persian pagan deities, *Marduk* and *Astarte.* Surely *Mordecai* knew the origin of these two names.

F and *v* are both labio-dentals and hence interchangeable.

Sinai[143] — סיני[143]

Biblical. Geographical name.
Name of the desert and the low mountain whereon Moshe, our teacher, received the written and the oral Torah. According to the Talmudic Sages, the word is a play on the Hebrew word sinah which means hatred. They claimed that the heathen nations held a sinah towards the Jewish People for being worthy of receiving the Torah on Sinai.

Sinaiya	סִינַאי
Sinaiye	סִנַאיַא
Shnaiya[144]	סִינַאיֶע
Shnaiye	שִׁנַאיַא[144]
	שִׁנַאיֶע

143. This is a symbolic name. Originally it was given to a great Talmudic scholar who was considered such a scholar that he had acquired the full knowledge of the Torah that was given to Jewry at Mount Sinai.
144. See footnote 93.

Theodoros[145] — תֵּיאדוֹרוֹס[145]

Greek.
"The gift of the Lord." A translation of Netaneil.

Todros[146]	תּוֹדְרוֹס[146]
Todras	תּוֹדְרַס
Todres	תּוֹדְרֶס
Todris	תּוֹדְרִיס

145. The Greek translation of *Netaneil* (*Nathaniel*).
146. All forms have become family names.

Toviyah (Tobias) — טוֹביה

Biblical. Zekharyahu, 6:10.
"The good I have is from God"—"God is good." One of the Kohanim (priests) in the time of Zekharyahu the Prophet.

Tuvyah	טוּבְיָה
Teve	טֶעבֶע
Tevel[147]	טֶעבֶעל[147]
Tevele[147]	טֶעבֶעלֶע[147]
Tevil[147]	טֶעבִיל[147]
Tevya	טֶעבְיַא
Tevye	טֶעבְיֶע
Tev	
Bueno[147a]	
Gutman[147a]	

147. See footnotes 30 and 394.
147a. *Bueno* is the Spainish equivalent for the Hebrew name *Toviyah*. *Bueno* itself was translated into the Yiddish (read German) name *Gutman*. See footnote 25. *Gutman*, and all variant spellings, derive from this form.

Tzvi (Hirsch) צְבִי (הִירשׁ)

Hebrew. Non-biblical.
"A deer." One of the male animal names. In German, hence in Yiddish, Hirsch.

Hirsch[148]	הִירשׁ[148]
Hersch	הֶערשׁ
Hirschel[149]	הִירְשׁל
Herschel[148]	הִירְשֶׁעל[149]
Herschil	הִירְשִׁיל
Hirtz[150, 151]	הֶערְשֶׁעל[148]
Hertz[151]	הֶערְשִׁיל
Hertzl	הִירץ[150]
Hertzel	הֶערץ[151]
Hertzke	הֶערְצל
Gershel[152]	הֶערְצֶעל
	הֶערְצְקֶע
	גֶערְשֶׁעל[152]

148. Two popular family names with variant spellings.
149. The Chief Rabbi of England, Solomon Hirschel (1762–1842), adopted his family name from his father's personal name—*Shlomoh ben Tzvi Hirschel.*
150. שׁ and צ are both dentals and hence interchangeable.
151. See footnote 109.
152. As there is no aspirant *H* in the Russian alphabet, the nearest is the *G*. The German-Jewish family name *H*urewitz often turned into *G*urewitz when a family bearing this name migrated to Russia.

Uri[153] אוּרִי[153]

Biblical. Shemot, 31:2.
"Enlightened"—"Intelligent." His son Betzaleil of the Tribe of Yehudah built the sanctuary in the desert.

Ure	אוּרֶע
Urele	אוּרֶעלֶע
Orlik	אוֹרְלִיק
Orcze	אוֹרְטשֶׁע

153. See footnote 141. With a slight phonetic variation, there derived the name *Orenstein* from this form.

Yaakov (Jacob) יַעֲקֹב

Biblical. Bereishit, 25:26.
"To heel"—"Grasp a heel." Yaakov, son of Yitzḥak and Rivkah, was the younger twin of Eisav (Esau). He entered the world after his brother, whilst grasping his heel. Yaakov was the father of the progenitors of the Tribes of Yisra'eil.

Yakov	יַעֲקֹבְמַאן[154]
Yakovman[154]	יַעֲקֹבְקָה[155]
Yakovka[155]	יַאקֶעל
Yokel	יַאקִיל
Yokil	יֶעקֶעל
Yekel	יֶעקִיל
Yekil	יַאנקֶעל[156]
Yankel[156]	יַאנקֶעלֶע
Yankele	קוּבַּא
Kuba	קוּבֶּע
Kube	קָאוֶועל
Kovel	קָאבִּי
Kuvel	קָאוִוי
Kovi	קָאבֶּעל
Kuli[157]	קוּבֶּעל
Culi	כּוּלִי[157]
Kule	כּוּלִי
Cule	גוּלקַא[158]
Gulka[158]	גוּלקֶע
Gulke	גוּלקָא[159]
Gulko[159]	קָאפֶּעל[160]
Koppel[160]	קָאפִּיל
Koppil	קָאפּוּל
Koppul	קֶערְפֶּעל[161]
Kerpel[161]	

154. The family name *Kaufman* derives from this form. (*Yakovman—Yakofman—Kofman—Kaufman.)* Some claim that this name derives from *Yekuti'eil. Yekuti'eil—Yekusi'eil—Yekusel—Kusel—Kus—Kusman—Kufman—Kaufman.* See footnote 36. See, also, last statement of 142 and first statement of 176.

155. The renowned author of the responsa *Noda Beyududa*, Rabbi Yeḥezkeil ben Yehudah-Leivi Landau of Prague (1717–1795), had a famous son, Rabbi *Yakovka* (1745–1822) who retained his childhood diminutive name form until his death. He was head of the Rabbinical court of Brod, Galicia (Poland).

156. The ע is properly pronounced with a combined glottal and velar expression. This causes the *n* to appear. The family name *Yankelevitch* is derived from this form.
157. An interesting diminutive. *Yakov—Yakuv—Yakuv'l—Kuvel—Kuvele—Kule*. Only the sound of the כ of the original name has remained intact. The other letters have been elided. In essence, it means that the diminutive suffix is all that is left of the name. *Culi* also became a family name.
158. *K* and *g* are both in the velar group and hence interchangeable.
159. *Gulko, Gulkes, Gulkin* are family names.
160. *P* and *b* are both labials and hence interchangeable. This and *Koppelman* are family names derivatives.
161. I cannot discover the phonetic dynamics for the entry of the ר into this diminutive form. It may have another origin.

Yeḥezkeil (Ezekiel) יחזקאל

Biblical. Ezekiel 1:3.
"The Lord will strengthen." Yeḥezkeil ben Buzzi the Kohan was a Prophet of God to the Jewish People in the Babylonian Diaspora. His prophecy started about seven years before the destruction of the First Holy Temple in Jerusalem.

Ḥezkel	חֶעזְקֶעל
Ḥeskel[162]	חֶעסְקֶעל[162]
Ḥaskel[163]	חַאסְקֶעל[163]
Ḥatzkel[162]	חַאצְקֶעל[162]
Ḥacze[162, 164]	חַאטְשֶׁע[164, 162]

162. ז, ס and צ (*z, s, tz* and *cz*) all belong to the dental group and hence are interchangeable.
163. *Haskel* (*Haskil*) became a family name.
164. See footnote 24.

Yeḥi'eil יחיאל

Biblical. Chronicles I, 15:18.
"The Lord lives"—"As the Lord lives," in the form of an oath. One of the seconds in command of the Levites, of those who were the keepers of the Gates of the Sanctuary.

Ḥiel	חִיֵאל
	כִיֵאל
Ikhel[165]	אִיכל[165]
Ikhil	אִיכִיל
Ikh'l Mikh'l[165, 166]	אִיכל מִיכל[166, 165]

165. The ח can be softened to ה (see footnote 63), and together with the initial י would form God's name. Hence the ה was hardened to כ and the first י was elided. The י is a weak letter to begin with and is elided from many names where it is the first letter.
166. See footnote 100.

Yehoshua (Joshua) יהושע

Biblical. Bamidbar, 13:8, 16.
"God will cause salvation." The spiritual and military leadership of the Jewish People were inherited by Yehoshua son of Nun on the death of Moshe. At first, his name was Hoshei'a, but when he was sent with the group to spy out the Land of Kenaan (Canaan), Moshe blessed his name with the addition of the Hebrew letter י which is the micro-cosmic form of God's name. He authored the book that carries his name.

Heishe[167]	הֵיישֶׁע[167]
Heishel	הֵיישֶׁעל
Heishek	הֵיישֶׁעק
Heishik	הֵיישִׁיק
Heshe[168]	הֶעשֶׁע[168]
Heshel[169]	הֶעשֶׁעל[169]
Heshke	הֶעשְׁקֶע
Hessel[170]	הֶעסִיל[170]
Hessil	הֶעסֶעל
Yehoshua Folk[171]	יְהוֹשֻׁעַ פּוֹלַק[171]
Yehoishua	שִׁיאַ[171a]
Shia[171a]	שִׁיעֶ[171a]
Shi'e[171a]	

167. See footnote 104.
168. See footnote 106.
169. Also a family name, but usually written in the German spelling *Heschel*. An interesting phenomenum happened with the family name of the *Apta-Kopyczynce* Chassidic Dynasty. The founder, Rabbi Avraham *Yehoshua Heshel* (1755–1825), adapted the diminutive form of his second personal name as his family name. The surname *Heschel* has remained till today with his descendants.
170. See footnote 93.
171. A plausible explanation for this combination of names has not been discovered. See footnote 117.
171a. ו (oo) is pronounced by many Jews as *I* (ai), especially in Poland and Ukraine.

Yehudah (Judah) יהודה

Biblical. Bereishit, 29–35.
"To thank God." The fourth son of Lei'ah born to Yaakov. King David was a direct male descendant of Yehudah. The Almighty blessed Yehudah that the Jewish kingship should eternally be of the Tribe that he progenited. The lion is the symbol of this Tribe.

Yehuda	יהוּדָא
Yuda	יוּדָא
Yude[172]	יוּדֶע[172]
Yudel	יוּדֶעל
Yiddel[173]	יִדֶעל[173]
Iddel	אִידֶעל
Yutka	אִידל
Yutke	יוּטְקָא
Yehudah Yudel	יוּטְקֶע
Yehudal Leib[174]	יהוּדָה יוּדֶעל
	יְהוּדָה לֵיבּ[174]

172. This diminutive form became the Germanic word *Jude* for the People of Israel. From *Jude* (pronounced *Yude*) was derived the word *Jew*.
173. Without the diminutive suffix *el*, we have the word *Yid*, or the less common *id*. The language name *Yiddish* (Judeo-German), derived from High Medieval German, was adopted by most Ashkenazi (European) Jews. It derived its name from the name *Yid*.
174. See footnote 7.

Yekuti'eil (Jekuthiel) יקותיאל

Biblical. Chronicles I, 4:18.
"One who harkens to the Lord"—"To keep his commandments."
Yekuti'eil was of the Tribe of Yehudah.

Yekutiel	קוּזל[175]
Yekusiel[175]	קוּזֶעל
Kozel[175]	קוּסְמַאן[175, 176, 177]
Kosman[175, 176, 177]	קוּזְמַאן[175, 177]
Kozman[175, 177]	קַאשְׁמַאן[175]
Koshman[175]	קַאשְׁמַאן[175, 177]
Kashman[175, 177]	קוּס
Kuss	קוּסֶעל[177a]
Kusel[177a]	קוּסְקֶע
Kuske	קוּשֶׁע
Kushe	קוּשְׁקֶע

Kushke
Kishke[177b]
Yiksil[177c]

קִישְׁקֶע[177b]
יֶקִיל[177c]

175. The Ashkenazi ת (*sav*—instead of *tav*), ז, ס, and שׂ are all dentals and hence interchangeable.
176. See footnote 36.
177. These forms became family names.
177a. The family name *Kusselevitz* derives from this form.
177b. This form developed into a family name in certain areas of Poland.
177c. This diminutive form is Ashkenazic in origin, based on the *sav* pronunciation of the tav. It developed thus: *Yekusiel—Yikusil— Yiksil.*

Yeshayahu (Isaiah) יְשַׁעְיָהוּ

Biblical. Yeshayahu, 1:1.
"The Lord saves." Prophet of God. His father Amotz was a brother of Amatzyah, King of Yehudah. He authored the book carrying his name.

Yeshaiyahu
Yeshaiyohu
Yeshaiya
Shaiya[178]
Shaika[179]
Shaike

יְשַׁעְיָה
שַׁעְיָה
שַׁאֲיָה[178]
שַׁאיקַא[179]
שַׁאיקֶע

178. The family name *Shaiyevitz* derived from this form.
179. The family name *Shaikevitz—Shaikovitz* derived from this form.

Yisra'eil[180] (Israel) יִשְׂרָאֵל[180]

Biblical. Bereishit, 32:25–29.
Contraction of two Hebrew words: Yasor—Nobly contended with and prevailed, Eil—God. "Nobly contended with God and prevailed." Yaakov's name was changed to Yisra'eil after he dreamt he had made battle with an Angel of God and prevailed. This triumphant dream battle of Yaakov is the symbolic contention with God that brought in its wake God's renaming him Yisra'eil.

Yisrael
Yisroel
Yisrol
Isser
Isserel

אִיסר
אִיסרל
אִיסרְלֶיין[181]
אִיסרְלִין[181]
אִיסרְלִישׁ[181]

Isserlein[181]	שׂרָאל
Isserlin[181]	סרָאל
Isserlis[181]	שׂרָאלִי
Srol	סרָאלִי
Sroli	סרָאלִיק
Srolik	סרָאלְקַא
Srolka	סרָאלְקֶ
Srolke	סרוּל
Srul	סרוּלִי
Sruli	סרוּלִישׁ[181a]
Srulish[181a]	סרוּלִיק
Srulik	סרוּלְקַא
Srulka	סרוּלְקֶע
Srulke	אוּלִי[182]
Ulli[182]	

180. In nearly all the diminutive forms of this name the initial י was elided. The suffix name of God (*el*) was also elided in each case.
181. Three diminutive forms became family names. The renowned Rabbinic Codifier who wrote additions to the *Shulkhan Arukh* (Code of Jewish Law), was named Rabbi Moshe Isserles. His father's Hebrew personal name was *Yisra'eil*. The shortened plus diminutive form is *Isserel*. Rabbi Moshe was called by a name denoting that he belonged to his father *Isserel*, and hence he was known as Rabbi Moshe *Isserel's*, which became condensed to *Isserles*. See footnote 135.

181a. See footnote 1c.

182. In this case only, the diminutive suffix and one letter of the original name remained. See also footnote 157.

Yissakhar[183] (Issachar) — יִשָּׂשכָר[183]

Biblical. Bereishit, 30:14-18.
Contraction of two Hebrew words: Yisa—"carry," Sekhar—"The rewarded one." Fifth son of Yaakov born of Lei'ah. The non-pronounced second letter שׂ in the Hebrew spelling, has no parallel in the whole of the Jewish Bible. Father of the Tribe carrying his name.

Yisokhar	יִשָׂכָר
Yisokhor	יִשָׂכָר בֶּער[184]
Isokhar	יִשָׂכָר בֶּרְמַאן[185]
Isokhor	
Yisokhor Ber[182]	
Yisokhor Berman[183]	

183. The double שׂשׂ is unique, and the second שׂ in speech was probably elided in ancient times.

184. *Ber* was originally coupled with *Yisokhor*. It is based on the Midrashic explanation of Genesis, 49:14–16 where *Yakov's* (the patriarch *Jacob)* blessings to his sons are recorded. In the blessing and personality description of *Yisokhor*, he is recorded as having to "bear a load." It is from the root "to bear" in German that this *Ber* in Yiddish derives. It has no connection (other than phonetic) with *Dov* meaning a bear (the animal). See also *Dov Ber*.

185. In this case the *man* of *Berman* could mean a *man* (a man who bears). The *man* of Yisokhor Ber*man* is possibly not a diminutive suffix as noted in footnote 36.

Yitzḥak (Isaac) יצחק

Biblical. Bereishit, 21:3, 6.
"Laughed"—"Rejoiced." Son of Avraham and Sarah. Sarah exclaimed, "The Lord has granted me a rejoicing; all those that will hear (of my giving birth to a boy) will rejoice on my account." At Yitzḥak's birth, Avraham was 100 years old, and Sarah was 90 years old. Yitzḥak was the second of the Jewish Patriarchs.

Yitzḥok	איציק[185a]
Itzik[185a]	איציג
Itzig	איצל
Itzel	איטשע
Icze	אייזיק[187, 186]
Aizik[186, 187]	אייזקמאן[189, 188, 187]
Aizikman[187, 188, 189]	אייזיקעל[187]
Aizikel[187]	זעקעל[190, 187]
Zekel[187, 190]	זעקל
Sekel[186, 187, 190]	סעקעל[190, 187, 186]
Aizlin[190a]	אייזלין[190]
Aizman[188, 189, 190a]	אייזמאן[190, 189, 188]

185a. See footnote 158.

186. צ, ז, ס are all dentals and hence interchangeable. *Aizik* is the German transliteration of *Itzḥak*.

187. These diminutive forms retain only the ק of the original names: *Aizik—Aizekel—Aizikman—Zekel—Sekel*.

188. See footnote 36.

189. These, with slight spelling variations, became family names.

190. The family names *Sichel*, *Zichel* and *Zichlin* derive from these forms.

190a. In these two extreme diminutive forms there is not left even one letter of the original phonetic structure of the name. Only the ז remains in exchange of the original צ.

Yoḥanan (Johanan—John) יוֹחנן

Biblical. Melakhim II, 25:23, Chronicles I, 3:15.
"The Lord graced" Son of Korei'ah, one of the chiefs of the warriors of the sons of Yehudah after the conquest of the Holy Land by the Chaldeans. Also, first born son of Yoshiyahu, son of Amon, King of Yehudah.

Yoḥonon	חַנַן[192, 191]
Yoḥanon	חָנָן
Ḥanan[191, 192]	חָאנִי[193]
Ḥonon	חָאנֶע
Ḥoni[193]	חָאנַא
Ḥone	
Ḥona	

191. See footnote 45.
192. See also *Elḥanan* which has identical diminutive forms.
193. The Talmud records the special metaphysical exploits of one of the greatest Talmudic Sages whose name was *Ḥoni Ha-Me'agil* (Ḥoni, the circle maker). In times of drought, he was want to draw a circle around himself and proclaim to the Almighty that he would not budge from his circle till the Almighty would have compassion on his children Yisra'eil, and send rain. It is recorded that this Sage was such a holy man that God invariably accepted his prayers, and rain fell immediately.

Yoseif (Joseph) יוֹסף

Biblical. Bereishit, 30:23-24.
"The Lord will add." Son of Yaakov. At his birth, his mother Raḥel exclaimed, "The Lord will add to me another son." And so it came to pass. She later bore to Yaakov another (the youngest), Binyamin. Yoseif was an interpreter of dreams. His brothers sold him into slavery in Egypt where, with the help of God, he eventually rose to great prominence. He became Viceroy of Egypt and, in that capacity he later received and helped his father Yaakov and his own brothers and their families to settle into Egypt. Thus started the Jewish exile of bondage in Egypt for 210 years.

Yosef[194, 195]	יוֹזְפַּא[195, 194]
Yozpa	יוֹזְפֶּע
Yozpe	יוֹסֶעל[196]

Yuzpa	יעסעל
Yuzpe	יעסיל
Yossel[196]	יוסקא[197]
Yessel	יוסקע
Yessil	יושקא[194]
Yoska[197]	יושקע
Yoske	יוסף יוסקא
Yoshka[194]	
Yoshke	
Yosef Yoske	

194. ז, שׂ, שׁ are dentals and hence interchangeable.
195. The פ and פּ are basically one letter in Hebrew. Note how the English alphabet carried over this principle from the Semitic language via the Greek: *P* as in *p*ull, and *Ph* as in *Ph*ilip.
196. The family names *Josselson* and *Jesselson* (*Yosselson* and *Yesselson*) derive from these forms.
197. The family names *Yoskewitz* and *Joskewitz* derive from these forms.

Ze'eiv (Zeev) זאב

Hebrew. Non-biblical.
" A wolf." One of the male animal names. In German, hence in Yiddish, Wolf—Velvel.

Wolf[198]	וואלף[198]
Wulf	וואלוול
Volf[198]	וואלוועל
Vulf	וועלוועל
Volvel	וועלוועלע
Velvel	וועלקא[199]
Velvele	וועלקע
Velka[199]	זאב וואלף
Velke	
Zeev Wolf	

198. *Wolf* is Yiddish (read Judeo-German). It also is a very common family name.* ב and פ are labio-dentals and *w* is a bi-labial. Phonetically they are all interchangeable.
199. *Volk* is the Slavic for *Wolf*, and *Velka* (*Velke*) are diminutives of the Russian translation. As ו and פ are both labio-dentals, *Velka* (*Velke*) would have evolved from the Slavic *Volk*. See footnotes 117 where the problem there stated may have some connection with *Volka* which could quite easily be pronounced as *Folka*.

Wolfish (*Wolf-ish*) is also a family name derivate. See footnote 1c.

* See footnote 195. As a result of this Hebrew letter having two consonant pronunciations, we end up with the family name derivative *Wolpe* (*Wolper*).

Zeide[200] — זיידע[200]

Yiddish.
"Grandfather"—"Old man." One of the amuletic names.

Zeide[201]	זֵיידְע[201]
Zeida	זֵיידַא
Zeidel[201]	זֵיידְעל[201]
Zeidil	זֵיידִיל
Zeidl	זֵיידל

200. This is an amuletic name. It expresses the parents' prayer that the infant boy should live to be old, and to be a grandfather. See also footnote 5, and see also *Alte* and *Boba*.
201. One of the early great Ḥassidic leaders was known as the *Spole Zeide*. His name was *Zeide* and he resided in the small township of Spole (Vohlynia district, Russia). There are hundreds of descendants of this *tzaddik* (saintly leader) whose family name are variations of the Yiddish. *Zeide, Seide, Seidel* are some variations of the name's spelling.

Zelig[202] — זעליג[202]

German.
"Happy one."

Zeligman[203, 204, 205]	זֶעלִיגְמַן[205, 204, 203]
Zelikman[204]	זֶעלִיגְמַאן
Zelle	זֶעלִיקְמַאן[204]
	זֶעלִיקְמַן
	זֶעלֶע

202. See footnote 11.
203. ג and ק both belong to the velar group and hence are interchangeable.
204. These forms are also family names.
205. See footnote 36.

Zundel[206] — זונדל[206]

German.
Sönlein. "Sonny boy"—"Small boy."

Zundel	זוּנְדְעל
Zundil	זוּנְדִיל

Zundul	זונדול

206. Very often coupled together with the name *Ḥanokh*. One could suggest the following: The biblical *Ḥanokh* was so righteous that he was the first of five who never died and who "was taken unto the Lord" whilst still alive. Maybe a child called *Zundel* is considered as free of sin and is thus likened to the original *Ḥanokh*. But, *Ḥanokh* derives from the root word "to educate"—"to raise correctly." The combination of *Ḥanokh Zundel* also suggests "to educate the child." When a Jewish boy is born, the first thought of the parents is concerned with the teaching (Ḥinukh) of their child—that he should learn Torah and be raised on its teachings. But more probably this combination is based on the admonition of the wise King Solomon found in the Book of Proverbs, 22:6 "Ḥanokh L'na'nar" (Educate the boy). The root of the Yiddish word *Zundel* is *Zun*. In German, Sohn and *del* is the diminutive suffix. *Zundel* is the Yiddish equivalent of the English "Sonny boy."

Zussya — זוסיא

German.
Züss—"Sweet one." Carried over into the Yiddish.

Zussye	זוסיע
Zussa	זוסא
Zusse	זוסע
Zissa[207]	זיסא[207]
Zisse	זיסע
Zissel[208]	זיסעל[208]
Zusha[209]	זושא[209]
Zushe	זושע
Zushel	זושעל
Zushya	זושיא
Zushye	זושיה
Zussman[210, 210a]	זושיע
Zusskind[210a]	זוסמאן[210a, 210]
Ziskind[210a]	זוסקינד[210a]
	זיסקינד[210]

207. These forms are also female names. See also *Zissa*.
208. See previous footnote.
209. שׂ and שׁ are both dentals and hence interchangeable.
210. *Man* is a diminutive suffix and does not necessarily mean a "man." See footnote 36. *Zussman* and *Sussman* both became family names.
210a. Notwithstanding that the diminutive form *Zussman* does not necessarily mean "a sweet man;" by etymological derivation (see footnote 36) the spoken word certainly does imply it. Hence, as there is no diminutive

base form of *Zusska—Ziska*, we must assume *Zusskind—Ziskind* are contra forms that were intentionally developed to specifically mean "a sweet child." *Kind* as a suffix is normally a phonetical aberrational extension of the suffix *kin*. *Züsskind* and *Ziskind* also became family names.

Female Personal Names

Adinah[211] — עדינה[211]

Biblical. Oral tradition.
"Gentile female." Wife of Leivi, son of Yaakov. Adinah was the great-granddaughter, through the male line, of Eiver. She was the progenitress of the Tribe of Leivi.

Ednah	עֶדְנַה
Adel[212]	אַדֶל[212]
Adela[213]	אַדֶלַה[213]
Eida[214]	אֵיידַא[214]
Eide	אֵיידֶע
Eidel	אֵיידֶעל
Eidil	אֵיידִיל
Eidul	אֵיידוּל
Eidela	אֵיידֶעלֶא
Eidele	אֵיידֶעלֶע

211. See also *Gentill*.
212. This is a simple translation into Yiddish. The rest are diminutives of various forms. The family names *Eidels* and *Edels* derive from this form.
213. Phonetically, this diminutive form is identical with the Teutonic *Adela* (Yiddish: *Eidela*) which means "of noble birth." This is no coincidence. Yiddish derives from High Medieval German, itself a derivative of the older Teutonic, and so both are of one origin. From the meaning "of noble birth" to the meaning of "gentle," there is no distance. A noble woman is, a priori, gentle.
214. There exists a biblical female name *Adah* (עָדָה) (Genesis, 4:19), but there is no proof of this being the root name for the very popular *Eidel*. *Adah* means "to pass by" or, according to some authorities, "an ornament."

Alte[215] — אלטע[215]

German.
"Old woman." From the German, hence in Yiddish. One of the amuletic names.

Alta	אַלְטַא
	אַלְטַה

215. One of the female amuletic names. See footnote 5. The ר (r) suffix differentiates the male form from the female form of the name. See also *Boba*, *Sabta*, *Zeide*, *Alter*.

Amelia[216] | אמעליא[216]

Teutonic.
"Busy"—"Energetic." Probably an equivalent of the Hebrew concept of Eishet Ḥayyil (Woman of Valour).

(Emeline)	אַמַלְיַא
Amalya	אַמַאלְיַא
Amalye	אַמַאלְיֶע
Malya	מַאלְיַא
Malye	מַאלְיֶע

216. Not directly a translation of any Hebrew name, but most probably based on King Solomon's description of the Jewish "Woman of Valour" (Proverbs, 31:10).

Asnat (Asenath) | אסנת

Biblical. Bereishit, 41:45.
"A thornbush"—"Bramble." From the Hebrew word Sneh. Adopted daughter of Potipherah the Egyptian priest of On. Asnat was born to Dinah, daughter of Yaakov, as a result of her having been raped by Shekhem. The trauma of the event, plus the fact that the rapist was an idolater, caused Dinah to reject her daughter. Dinah's brother Shimon raised the baby for a while, but then he, too, rejected her. Tradition has recorded that he hid the child under a thornbush, hence her name, intending her to be found. Potiphera's servants found her and took her to their master who raised her. Jewish tradition always ascribes parenthood to the one who raises the child. Asnat married her uncle Yoseif and bore him two sons, Menashe and Efrayim.

Like the name Sinai, which our Sages claim has the word Sinah, hatred, as its root, it is possible that Asnat also has Sinah as its root, and it thus may infer the mother Dinah's hatred for her daughter born under such traumatic conditions. It is also possible that Asnat is an Egyptian name, since in Egyptian Asenath means "Belonging to God" or "Belonging to Neth" where Neth is an Egyptian goddess.

Osnas[217]	אָסְנַאס[217]
Asnas	אַסְנֶעס
Asnes	אַסְנַא
Asna	אַסְנַה
Asne	אַסְנֶע

217. Derived immediately from the Ashkenazi pronunciation of the תּ (t) as a ת (s).

Avigayil (Abigail) אביגיל

Biblical. Shmuel I, 25:3, Chronicles I, 2:16.
Contraction of two Hebrew words: Avi "father of" (to create or induce) and Gil "joyous stirrings"—"happenings." Widowed wife of Naval who married King David. Also, King David had a sister with the same name as this wife.

Avigaiyil
Avigal
Avigali
Ogla[218]
Igla
Ogle
Igle
Oglin
Ogush[219, 219a]
Ogushe[219]

אֲבִיגַל
אֲבִיגַלִי
אוֹגְלַא[218]
אִיגְלַא
אוֹגְלַה
אִיגְלַה
אוֹגְלֶע
אִיגְלֶע
אוֹגְלִין
אָגוּשׁ[219a, 219]
אָגוּשֶׁע[219]

218. An interesting example of elision without any apparent reason. *(Avigaiyil—Avigal—Avigali—Ovigali—Ogla—Ogle—Igla—Igle)*
There is a possibility of phonetic coincidence with this diminutive form. In Numbers, 26:33 it states that one of the daughters of *Tzelafḥad* was *Ḥaglah* (Ashkenazi: *Ḥoglah*). As explained in footnote 63 the ח can be softened to a ה, and on the basis of what was discussed in footnote 1, *Ḥoglah* becomes *Ogla*. See also footnote 9.
219. The family names *Ogushewitz* and *Ogushwitz* derive from these diminutive names.
219a. See footnote 1c.

Batyah בתיה

Biblical. Chronicles I, 4:17-18.
"Daughter of God." Daughter of the Pharoah of the Egyptian bondage. It was she who had Moshe withdrawn from the reeds of the Nile River and who gave him his name and cared for him. Batyah became a righteous proselyte to Judaism and left Egypt together with all the Jews at the Exodus. She married Mered, son of Ezra of the Tribe of Yehudah. It seems that Batyah was given

this name after she became Jewish.

Basya[220]	בַּסְיַא[220]
Basye	בַּאסְיֶע
Basel	בַּאסֶעל
Besel	בֶּעסֶעל
Beserel	בֶּעסֶערְעל
Basha[221]	בַּאשַׁא[221]
Bashe	בַּאשֶׁע
Bashala	בַּאשַׁאלַא
Bashale	בַּאשַׁאלֶע
Basharel	בַּאשַׁארֶעל
Batka[222]	בַּאטְקַא[222]
Batke	בַּאטְקֶע
Pasha[223]	פַּאשַׁא[223]
Pashe	פַּאשַׁה
Pesa	פַּאשֶׁע
Pese	פֶּעסַא
Pesya	פֶּעסֶע
Pesye	פֶּעסְיַא
Pesha	פֶּעסְיֶע
Peshe	פֶּעשַׁא
Peshya	פֶּעשֶׁע
Peshye	פֶּעשְׁיַא
	פֶּעשְׁיֶע

220. See footnote 217. See next footnote.

221. The ת and the שׂ are both dentals and hence interchangeable. Some authorities claim that this form derives from the female name *Batsheva*.

222. An interesting example of a Sefardi-Ashkenazi pronunciation mixture. The ת remained Sefardi, and the *ka* diminutive suffix is purely Ashkenazi (Slavic based). *Batkin* and *Patkin* are family names derived from this form.

223. ב and פ are both bi-labial and hence interchangeable.

Bilhah בִּלְהָה[224]

Biblical. Bereishit, 30:3-8.
"To act rashly out of confusion." Maid servant of Raḥel, wife of Yaakov. Legal concubine of Yaakov. Bilhah bore to Yaakov, Dan and Naftali who progenitored the Tribes carrying their names.

Bilah	בִּלָה
Bileh	בִּילַה

Billa[224]	בִּילַא[224]
Bille	בִּילֶע
Beila[225]	בֵּיילַא[225]
Beile	בֵּיילֶע
Beilah	בֵּיילַה
Beilka[225a]	בֵּיילְקַא[225a]
Beilke	בֵּיילְקֶע

224. This unique Hebrew spelling of double הה ended up with the elision of both letters. See footnote 1.
225. The Spanish and Italian name *Bella* (beautiful) has no connection whatsoever with the biblical name *Bilhah* whose root means "confusion." This phonetic similarity, and its meaning of "beautiful," made it a popular name for one with the name *Bilhah*. See also *Yaffa*. The Hebrew female name *Bilhah* was very popular in pre-expulsion Spain, and it permitted its bearer to disguise it among the Gentiles by using the name *Bella* (beautiful). The family name *Beilin* derives from this form.
225a. The family name *Belkin* derives from this form.

Boba[226] — בּאבּא[226]

Slavic.
"Grandmother." One of the amuletic names. Adopted into Yiddish.

Bobe	בָּאבֶּע
Bobale	בָּאבַּאלֶע
Bobala	בָּאבֶּעלֶע
Bobele	בָּאבִּינצ׳קַא
Bobela	בָּאבִּינצ׳קֶע
Bobinczke	
Bobinczka	

226. One of the female amuletic names. See footnote 5. See also *Alte, Sabta, Zeide, Alter*.

Bodhana[227] — באדהאנא[227]

Ukranian. Hebrew.
"God graced." Bod—God; Hana, from the Hebrew word Ḥannah—Grace.

Bodhane	בָּאדהַאנֶע
Bodhana	בָּאדהַאנַא
Bodana	בָּאדַאנַא

Bodane	בָּאדַאנֶע
Bodnia	בָּאדנִיַא
Bodnie	בָּאדנִיֶע
Bodna	בָּאדנַא
Bodne	בָּאדנֶע

227. The *Bod* part of the name means *God* in Ukrainian. The *Hana* part is our well-known Hebrew *Ḥannah*, but the ח has been softened to ה, and eventually it has been elided. See footnote 63.

Breina[228] [228]בריינא

German.
Bräune. Adjective: feminine brown colour. Into Lithuanian and White Russian Yiddish accent. One of the five female names referring to complexion, eyes or hair.

Breine	בְּרֵיינַה
Breindel[229]	בְּרֵיינֶע
Breindil	[229]בְּרֵיינדֶעל
Broina	בְּרֵיינדִיל
Broine	ברוֹינַא
Broindel[229]	ברוֹינֶע
Broindil	[229]ברוֹינדֶעל
Bruna	ברוֹינדִיל
Brune	ברוּנַא
Brundel[229]	ברוּנֶע
Brundil	[229]ברוּנדֶעל
	ברוּנדִיל

228. There are at least five Ashkenazi female names that refer to colour, complexion, eyes or hair.*
Breina – Brown (Lithuanian, Yiddish), hair or eyes.
Czarna – Black (Slavic languages), brunette or eyes.
Gelleh – Yellow (Yiddish), blonde or gingy colour.
Gruna – Green (Judeo-German, Old Yiddish), eyes.
Roza – Rose (Yiddish), Redhead or rosy cheeks.

229. As explained in the introduction, one of the Old German diminutive suffixes for names ending with a vowel plus *n*, is *del*. This phenomenum will be met with many times.

* A few hundred years ago there was in use a personal name *Shaḥor* (Hebrew: black) for a male brunette. The Yiddish (Judeo-German) translation *Schwarz* took over, and it ended up also as *Schwarzman* both eventually becoming well-known family names (spelled in various ways). See footnote 36. The original

personal name *Shaḥor* also continued as a family name of an illustrious Rabbinic family which still exists today. They hailed from Prague.

Bunah[230] בּוּנָה[230]

Spanish.
Buena (good) in feminine gender. The independent translation equivalent of the Hebrew Tovah.

Buna[231]	בּוּנַא[231]
Buneh	בּוּנֶע
Bunya	בּוּנְיַא
Bunye	בּוּנְיֶע
Bunalah	בּוּנַלַא
Bunale	בּוּנַלֶע
Bundel	בּוּנדל
Bunina[232]	בּוּנִינַא[232]
Buninne	בּוּנִינֶע
Bunczeka	בּוּנצְ׳קַא
Bunczeke	בּוּנצְ׳קֶע
Bubuna[232]	בּוּבּוּנַא[232]
Bina[233]	בִּינַא[233]
Bineh	בִּינֶע

230. The Spanish for *Tovah* which could imply that the name is of pre-expulsion vintage.
231. The family name *Bunin—Boonin—Bounin*, derives from this form.
232. The doubling of consonants is a diminutive structure; in one form the נ is doubled, and in the other form the ב is doubled.
233. This diminutive form has no connection with the female Hebrew name *Binah* which means "understanding." It is a phonetical coincidence.

Czarna[234] טשׁארנא[234]

Slavic.
"Black." Infers a brunette or a woman with black eyes. One of the five female names referring to colour, complexion, eyes or hair.

Czarne	טשׁאַרנֶע
Czarni	טשַׁארנִי
Tzarna	צַארנַא
Tzarne	צַארנֶע
Tzarina[235]	צַארִינַא[235]

Tzarine	צאַרינֶע

234. One of the colour group. See footnote 228.
235. A phonetic caprice that arrives at the Russian word for a queen. Tzar—czar derives from the Latin *Caesar* which in Slavic languages ended up as czar or tzar. This form is not a translation of *Malkah*.

Devorah (Deborah) דבוֹרה

Biblical. Bereishit, 35:8, Shoftim, 4:4.
"A bee." The wet nurse of Rivkah, the wife of Yitzḥak. Devorah was the daughter of Utz, son of Naḥor. Naḥor was the brother of Avraham. Utz was the brother of Bethueil, son of Naḥor. Rivkah was Bethueil's daughter. Hence, Devorah was an older first cousin to Rivkah. Devorah never married. The other and more famous one was Devorah, the Prophetess of God. She was the wife of Lapidot.

The name may have originally been given to a baby girl because her crying may have had a buzzing or humming sound of a bee.

Dvoira, Dvora	דוואָרַא
Dvoire, Dvore	דוואָרֶע
Dvoirel, Dvorel	דוואָרֶעל
Dvoirele, Dvorele	דוואָרֶעלֶע
Dvoirale, Dvorale	דוואָרַאלֶע
Dvoirka, Dvorka[235a]	דוואָרקַא
Dvoirke, Dvorke[235a]	דוואָרקֶע
Dveira[236]	דווֵיירַא[236]
Dveire	דווֵיירֶע
Veira	וֵיירַא
Veire	וֵיירֶע
Vera[237]	וֵערַא[237]
Dvosha[238]	דוואָשׁא[238]
Dvoshe	דוואָשֶׁע
Dvoshel	דווֹשֶׁעל
Dvoshka	דוואָשקַא
Dvoshke	דוואָשקֶע

235a. The family names *Dvorkes* and *Dvorkin* are derived from this form.
236. See footnote 104.
237. A phonetic coincidence that *Dveira* diminutises to *Vera* which comes from the Latin *Veritas* which means truth. There is no etymological connection.
238. The *sh* is a diminutive insertion. See footnote 1c. In this case, the insertion was probably intentional, because the *el* and the *ka* (*ke*) are

only Germanic and Slavic diminutive additions. The root of these diminutives is *Dvosh* (Sefardi pronunciation: *Dvash*). *Dvosh* is the Hebrew for "honey." This diminutive form of the name *Devorah*, a bee, is probably not a phonetic coincidence.

Dobah — דוֹבה

Hebrew. Non-biblical.
"A female bear."

Doba	דָאבַה
Dobe	דָאבַא
Dobka[239]	דָאבֶע
Dobke	[239]דָאבקַא
	דָאבקֶע

239. The family name *Dobkin* derives from this Slavic diminutive form.

Drozha — דראז׳א

Slavic.
"My dear little one."

Drozhe	דראָז׳ע
Drozna[240]	[240]דראָז׳נַא
Drozne	דראָז׳נֶע
Dreiza[241]	[241]דרֵייזַא
Dreize	דרֵייזֶע
Dreizel	דרֵייזֶעל
Dreizil	דרֵייזִיל
Drezel[242]	[242]דרֶעזִיל
Drezil	דרֶעזִיל

240. The presence or absence of the נ is dependent on local Slavic phonetics.
241. The Slavic *zh* and the ז are both dentals and hence interchangeable.
242. Russian phonetics are such, that the *o* (as in h*o*t) and the *e* (as in p*e*g) often interchange.

Esteir (Esther) — אסתר

Biblical. Esteir, 2:7
Ancient Persian. "A tree used in idolatrous rites"—"Fertility symbol." In Hebrew—Asheirah. Queen Esteir's Hebrew name was Hadassah. Through her, the Almighty brought salvation to the Jewish People. She was God fearing, beautiful and wise. When her parents died, Mordekhai, her cousin, adopted and raised her

like his own child. Because the salvation wrought for the Jews, recorded in the Book of Esteir, was brought about with the Almighty in the background, our Sages claim that the name Esteir actually derives from the Hebrew word seiter (secret or hidden.) The inference is that God's immediate presence was hidden. The Megilat Esteir carries her name.

Ester	אסתרינא
Estrina	טרינא
Trina	טרינע
Trinne	טריינא[243]
Treina[243]	טריינע
Treine	טריינדל
Treindel	אסתרעל
Esterel	אסתריל
Esteril	סטערנא
Sterna	סטרנע
Sterne	סטערעל
Sterel	סטערליין[244]
Sterlein[244]	סטערלין
Sterlin	עטע
Etta	עטא
Ette	עטעל
Ettel	עטיל
Ettil	עטקא[245]
Etka[245]	עטקע
Etke	עסא
Essa	עסע
Esse	עסקא[246]
Eska[246]	עסקע
Eske	איטא[247]
Itta[247]	איטע
Itte	איטקא
Itka	איטקע
Itke	

243. The family name *Trainer—Treiner* derives from this form.
244. The family name *Sterling* derives from these forms. See footnote 135.
245. The family name *Etkin* derives from this form.
246. The family name *Eskin* derives from this form. See also footnote 389.
247. A phonetic abberation. *Itta*, *Itte*, *Itka* and *Itke* are also diminutive forms of *Yehudit*. See also footnote 9. The *e* (like in egg) and the *i* (like in b*i*g) can phonetically interchange. See also *Miriam*—Mirke and Merke.

Freida פריידא

Derived from the German "Freude."
"Joy"—"Satisfaction"—"Comfort."

Freide	פרֵיידֶע
Freidel[248]	פרֵיידֶעל[248]
Freidil	פרֵיידִיל
Freidka[248]	פרֵיידקַא[248]
Freidke	פרֵיידקֶע
Frada	פרַאדַא
Frade	פרַאדֶע
Fradel	פרַאדֶעל
Fradil	פרַאדִיל
Fradka[248]	פרַאדקַא[248]
Fradke	פרַאדקֶע

248. The name derived from the German word *freude*, meaning "joy." As explained in footnote 104, the *oi* sound is pronounced by some Jews as *ei*.

It is a female translation of the male name *Simḥah*. The family names *Freides*, *Freidin*, *Freidlin*, *Freidkes* and *Freidkin* derive from these forms. Also, *Fradkes* and *Fradkin* derive therefrom.

Frieda פרידא

Old High German.
"Peace"—"Tranquility"—"Harmony." Frederica was the full original form.

Friede[249]	פרִידֶע[249]
Friedel	פרִידֶעל
Friedil	פרִידִיל
Friedka	פרִידקַא
Friedke	פרִידקֶע

249. The original Old High German form was *Frederica*, and the diminutive thereof is *Frieda*. *Friede* is the German word for "peace," and hence, this may be an international female translation of the male name *Shalom*. The family name *Friedman—Freedman* derives from *Friede* and has no connection with the meaning "a freed man" (suggesting prior serfdom). See footnote 36.

Frommet פרוּמעט

Old provincial French.
"A certain species of grape."

Froma פראָמַא
Fromme פראָמֶע
Frommel פראָמֶעל
Frommetel פראָמֶעטֶעל
Fruma[250] פרוּמַא[250]
Frumme פרוּמֶע
Frummel פרוּמֶעל
Frumka[251] פרוּמקַא[251]
Frumke פרוּמקֶע
Frummet פרוּמֶעט
Frummetel פרוּמֶעטֶעל

250. Only through ignorance of the origin and meaning of the word was the mistake made to presume that the name meant in Yiddish "pious one." The mistake was further compounded by women in Israel who Hebracised their names from *Fruma* to *Ḥassidah* (pious one). Even today, some women have retained the older form *Frommet* or *Frummet*.*
251. The family names *Frumkes* and *Frumkin* derive from this diminutive form.

* There are some who claim that this name derives from the German word *Frohmut* ("joy" in German) and that it was a translation of *Simḥah*. See footnote 248. This is highly improbable, as this name was used exclusively by woman, and *Frohmut* is masculine gender.

Gelleh[252] געלע[252]

Yiddish.
"Yellow." Refers to a blond or a light redhead. One of the five female colour names. Derived from the German word *gelb* (yellow).

Gellah גֶעלַא
Galyah[253] גַאליַא[253]
Galleh גַאלֶע
Hellah הֶעלַא
Helleh[254] הֶעלֶע[254]
Hallah הַאלַא
Halleh הַאלֶע

252. See footnote 228.
253. This is a Russified form of the Yiddish.

254. The family name *Heller* derives from this form. It would be correct to assume that the original personal name form was *Helleh* and that the ה turned into a ג in Russia. See footnote 152.

Genana[255] | גננא[255]

Old High German.
"Grandmother"—"Old woman" when used as a Jewish name. Basically, it can also be a grandfather or old man. One of the amuletic names.

Genaneh	גנֲנֶע
Genena	גֶעֶנֶעֶנַא
Genenneh	גֶעֶנֶעֶנֶע
Genendel[256]	גֶנֶענדֶעל[256]
Genendil	גֶנֶענדִיל
Ginesha[257]	גִינֶעשַׁא[257]
Gineshe	גִינֶעשֶׁע
Nenneh	נֶעֶנֶע
Nennel	נֶעֶנֶעל

255. Another amuletic name. See footnote 5.
256. See footnote 229. The family name *Gendel* may be a contracted derivative of this form.
257. The *sha* and *she* suffixes are the female diminutive variations of the male *ish* and *ush*. See footnote 1c.

Gentille[258] | גנטילע[258]

Old French.
"A gentle female."

Gentila	גְ׳ענטִילַא
Gentelle	גֶענטִילֶע
Yentileh[258a]	יֶענטִילֶע[258a]
Yenteleh	יֶענטֶעלֶע
Yentlin	יֶענטלִין
Yente[259]	יֶענטֶע[259]
Yenta	יֶענטַא
Yentel	יֶענטֶעל

258. Some authorities claim that *Gentille* is a direct translation of the Hebrew female name *Adinah* (gentle one). But there is no evidence that the female name *Adinah* was in use during the early medieval period. The

name was probably just borrowed and used by Jews.

258a. The *y* as a consonant; the *j* and *g*, as in *j*ump and *g*iant, are interchangeable from some languages to others as one phonetic system has to cope with another. As Dutch language has no equivalent of the English *j*, a Dutchman will say pi*y*ama for py*j*ama.

Likewise, the soft *g* of *Gentille*; in Yiddish turned into a *y*. To attain *j* in Yiddish, one has to write דז׳ (a *dalet* and a *zayyin* with an apostrophe—*dzh*). [or ג׳ with an apostrophe as used in modern Hebrew—Ed.]

Ironically, pure Hebrew has two *gimmels* (ג)—one hard and one soft, pronounced like in *g*reat and in *g*iant. Due to the wandering from one European exile to another, Ashkenazi Jewry's phonetics were influenced by the host countries' languages, and they lost the original *j* sound of Hebrew. Many Sefardim retained the two *gimmels* in their Hebrew because it exists in Arabic, their usual host countries' language.

259. The most abused female Jewish name. This was caused by Yiddish writers who capriciously selected this name for the most unsympathetic female character in their romance novels. Because of this, the name which means gentle has been turned into a most negative name.

Gisse גיסע

Old High German. Old German.
"Geisel"—hostage; "Geiss"—a doe.

Gissa[260]	גִיסַא[260]
Gissel	גִיסֶעל
Gissela	גִיסֶעלַא
Gissele	גִיסֶעלֶע
Gisha[261]	גִישַׁא[261]
Gishe	גִישֶׁע
Gizza[262]	גִיזַא[262]
Gizze	גִיזֶע

260. The family name *Gissin* derives from this form.
261. The *s* and the *sh* are both dentals and hence interchangeable. The family name *Gishin* derives from this form. As the letters *g* and *k* are both in the velar group, the name also developed into *Kishin*.
262. *S*, *sh* and *z* are all dentals and hence interchangeable.

Golda גאלדא

Yiddish.

"Gold"—"Golden personality." Derived from the German gold.

Goldeh	גָאלדֶע
Goldeleh	גָאלדֶעלֶע
Goldinchke	גָאלדִינצ´קֶע
Zlota[263]	זלָאטַא[263]
Zlotte	זלָאטֶע
Zlotka[263a]	זלָאטקַא[263a]
Zlotke	זלָאטקֶע

263. The Polish word for "gold." Zlota is the name of a Polish gold coin. A simple translation to the Yiddish.

263a. The family name *Zlotkin—Slotkin* derives from this form.

Notwithstanding that the expression "Goldilocks," in English, decribes a woman with blonde hair, it cannot be established that the name *Golda*, in Yiddish, is one of the colour group (see footnote 228). It most probably infers "a woman with a *golden* character," a derivative name based on the description of a virtuous woman mentioned in Proverbs, 31:10.

Gruna[264] גרוּנא[264]

German.
"Green." Derived from the German *Grün*. Either describing a jealous female nature or the colour of a woman's eyes. One of the five female colour names.

Grune	גרוּנֶע
Grunia	גרוּנְיַא
Grunie	גרוּנְיֶע
Grina	גרִינַא
Grineh	גרִינֶע

264. See footnote 228. Some authorities claim that this female name and the male name *Gronum* both derive from the Greek name *Geronimus* and that the family name *Groner* derives therefrom. Geronimus in Greek means "an old one." That would imply that the name belongs to the amuletic group (see also: *Alter, Alte, Boba, Zeide, Sabta, Saba*, etc.) There is no proof that the name was used amuletically at the early period that the name *Geronimus* was first used.

Ḥaiyyah חַיָה

Hebrew. Non-biblical.
"Life"—"Living." Also used as an amuletic name.

Ḥaiyyah
Ḥaiyala
Ḥaiyalle
Ḥeika[272]
Ḥeike
Ḥeikalle
Ḥeikelle
Keila[273]
Keile
Keika
Keike
Keikela[274]
Keikelle

חַיילָא
חַיילֶע
חַייקָא[272]
חַייקֶע
חַייקָאלֶע
חַייקֶעלֶע
קֵיילָא[273]
קֵיילֶע
קֵייקָא
קֵייקֶע
קֵייקֶלָא[274]
קֵייקֶלֶע

272. The family name *Ḥaikin—Ḥeikin* derives from this form.
273. See footnote 65. In this case, the ח turned into a ק.
The phonetics of some languages do not possess the *kh* like in *Khartoum*, nor *ch* like in the Scottish loch. Both *kh* and *ch* end up as a *k*. Apparently individuals have this phonetic problem irrespective of their mother tongue.
274. See footnote 232.

Ḥaiyyah Esteir — חַיָה אֶסתֶּר

Non-biblical and biblical.
The combination of the names Ḥaiyyah and Esteir. See each name separately.

Ḥaiyetta[275] — חַייעֶטָא[275]
Ḥaiyetteh — חַייעֶטֶע

275. A rare form created by the phonetic contraction of two names into one.

Ḥaiyyah Henne[276] — חַיָה הֶענֶע[276]

Non-biblical and biblical.
The combination of the names Ḥaiyyah and Ḥannah. See each name separately.

Ḥaiyenna[277] — חַייעֶנָא[277]
Ḥaiyenneh — חַיינֶנֶע

276. See *Ḥannah*. *Henne* is a diminutive form of *Ḥannah*.
277. See footnote 275.

Ḥannah[266] חנה

Biblical. Shmueil I, 1:2.
"Gracious"—" Graceful." Mother of the Prophet Shmueil. Wife of Elkanah. By her piety and silent prayers to the Almighty, she was blessed with a son after years of being barren.

Ḥanna	חַאנַא
Ḥanne	חַאנֶע
Ḥancze	חַאנטשֶע
Ḥaniczka	חַאניטשקַא
Ḥaniczke	חַאניטשקֶע
	חַאנטשֶעקֶע
Hana[267]	הַאנַא[267]
Hanne	הַאנֶע
Henna	הֶענַא
Henne	הֶענֶע
Henka[267a]	הֶענקַא[267a]
Henke	הֶענקֶע
Henya	הֶעניַא
Henye	הֶעניֶע
Ḥanala	חַאנַאלַא
Ḥanalle[268]	חַאהַאלֶע
Ḥanela	חַאנֶעלַא
Ḥanelle	חַאנֶעלֶע
Genya[268a]	גֶעניַא[268a]
Genye	גֶעניֶע

266. The Sefardi female name *Gracia* is a simple Spanish translation of the Hebrew.
267. See footnote 65.
267a. The family name *Henkin* derives from this form.
268. The family name *Hannales* derives from these forms.
268a. See footnote 152.

Ḥavah (Eve) חוה

Biblical. Bereishit, 3:20.
"Gives life." From the word ḥayyah (life). The Torah tells us of Adam, that on the formation of his wife, "Her name he called Ḥavah, because she was the mother of all living."

Ḥaveh[269]	חַאוַוא[269]
Ḥavel	חַאווע
Ḥaval	חַאוַואל

Ḥavala[270]	חַאווֶעל
Ḥavaleh	חַאווַאלַא[270]
Ḥavela	חַאווַאלֶע
Ḥaveleh	חַאווֶעלַא
Ḥavka[271]	חַאווֶעלֶע
Ḥavke	חַאווקַא[271]
	חַאווקֶע

269. The family name *Ḥavin* derives from this form.
270. From this group there derives the family name *Ḥavlin*.
271. From these forms there derives the family name *Ḥavkin*.

Hadassah[265] הדסה[265]

Biblical. Esteir, 2:7.
"Myrtle." One of the four botanical spices used together with the palm, etrog and willows during the Festival of Sukkot. It was the Hebrew name of Queen Esteir.

Hodas	הָאדַאס
Hodes	הָאדֶעס
Hadas	הָאדַא
Hades	הָאדֶע
Hoda	הָאדִיַא
Hoddeh	הָאדִיֶע
Hodiah	הָאדֶעל
Hodel	הָאדִיל
Hodil	

265. The Hebrew name of *Queen Esteir*. See *The Book of Esteir*, 2:7. Also see last statement of footnote 142.

Illa אִילַא

Aramaic.
"Superior quality"—"The best."

Ella[278]	עֶלַא
Elleh	עֶלֶע
Ilka	אִילקַא
Ilke	אִילקֶע
Elka[279]	עֶלקַא
Elke	עֶלקֶע
Ellush[279a]	עֶלוּש
Illush	אִילוּש

278. See last comment in footnote 247 concerning the phonetic interchangeability of *e* and *i*.
279. The family names *Elkin* and *Elkind* derive from this form.
279a. See footnote 1c.

Ketziah[280] — קְצִיעָה[280]

Biblical. Iyyov, 42:14.
A special species of cinnamon used in the incense offerings in the Sanctuary and the Holy Temple. One of the three daughters of Iyyov (Job).

Katzia[281]	קַאצִיאַ[281]
Katzie	קַאצִּיֶע
Kassia[282]	קַאסִּיאַ[282]
Kassie	קַאסִּיֶע
Khassia[283]	כַאסִּיֶא[283]
Khassie	כַאסִּיֶע
Hassia[283]	חַאסִּיאַ[283]
Hassieh	חַאסִּיֶע
Haska[284]	חַאסקַא[284]
Haskeh	חַאסקֶע
Hasha[282]	חַאשַׁא[282]
Hasheh	כַאשֶׁע
	כַאשַׁא
	כַאשֶׁע

280. *Cassia* was one of the ingredients in the incense offering in the Temple in Jerusalem.
281. The family name *Katzin* possibly derives from this name form or from the Hebrew *Katzin* meaning "an officer of the community."
282. צ, ס and שׂ all belong to the dental group and are hence interchangeable.*Ketziah—Kessiah—Kassiah—Cassia*.Manynon-Ashkenazi Jews, especially Yemenites, always pronounce the Hebrew letter צ as *saddik*.
283. See footnote 65. In this case the ק turned into a כ and ח. See also footnote 273.
284. The family name *Haskin* derives from this form.

Kuna[285] — קוּנַא[285]

Old Spanish.
"A cradle"—"Childish"—"Infantile."

Kune[286]	קוּנֶע[286]

Kunya	קוּנַיא
Kunye	קוּניֶע

285. See also the male name *Kuni*.
286. The family name *Kunin* is derived from this form.

Lei'ah (Leah) לאה

Biblical. Bereishit, 29:23.
"Weak"—"Sickly." The older daughter of Lavan (Laban) the Aramaen (a Semitic Tribe). First wife of Yaakov. She is buried with her husband in the tomb of the Patriarchs in Ḥevron.

Lei'l	לֵאה´ל
Leiale	לֵאַהלֶע
Leika[287]	לֵייקַא[287]
Leike	לֵייקֶע
Leiyinka	לֵאיינקַא
Leiyinke	לֵאיינקֶע
Leicza	לֵייטשַׁא
Leicze	לֵייטשֶׁע
Leitza	לֵייצַא
Leitze	לֵייצֶע

287. The family names *Leikes* and *Leikin* derive from this form.

Lieba[288] לִיבַּא[288]

German, hence into Yiddish.
"Loved one"—"Lovable."

Liebe
Liba
Libbe
Liebel
Libbel
Liberel[289]
Liberil
Livsha[290]
Livshe
Lifsha[290]
Lifshe
Luba[291]

לִיבֶּע
לִיבֶּעל
לִיבֶּערֶעל[289]
לִיבֶּערִיל
לִיבשַׁא
לִיבשֶׁע[290]
לִיפשַׁא[290]
לִיפשֶׁע
לוּבַא[291]

288. See also the male name *Lieber*.

289. See footnotes 65 and 85.

290. ב, which is in the bi-labial group, and ב are one letter in Hebrew; and ב and פ are both labio-dentals. Hence, all three are interchangeable. This is *not* the root of the family name Lifshitz which is derived from the names of two towns, Loeschutz and Leibesch.

291. See footnote 85.

Maḥlah — מחלה

Biblical. Bamidbar, 26:33.
"Golden bangles"—"Jewellry." From the root word Hali. One of the daughters of Tzelafḥad.

Maḥle[292]	מַחלָא
Makhla	מַחלֶע[292]
Makhle[292]	מַאחלָא
	מַאחלֶע[292]
	מַאכלָא
	מַאכלֶע[292]

292. The family names *Machlis—Machles—Makhlis—Makhles* derive from these forms.

Malkah[293, 293a] — מלכה[293a, 293]

Hebrew. Non-biblical.
"A queen."

Malkala	מַלכַּלָה
Malkale	מַלכְּלָא
Malkela	מַלכְּלֶע
Malkele	סוּלטַנָה[294]
Sultana[294]	סוּל
Sul	סוֹל
Sol	

293. Not to be confused with the independent name *Milkah*, which has identical spelling in Hebrew.

293a. The family name *Malkin* derives from the original name form.

294. An Old Spanish translation name that is still popular with Sefardi women.

Margolah — מרגולה

Semitic. Non-biblical.

"A pearl"—"A precious stone."

Margola	מַארגוֹלַא
Margoleh	מַארגוֹלֶע
Margoliyah	מַארגָאלִיַא
Margolit	מַארגָאלִיע
Margolis[295]	מַרגוֹלִית[295]

295. The well-known family names *Margolioth*, *Margoliot*, *Margolies*, etc. derive from this diminutive form. See also *Penninah*.

Masheh[296] — מאשה[296]

Hebrew. Non-biblical.
A novel feminine form of Moshe.

Mashah	מַשַׁה
Masha	מַשַׁא
Mashe	מַשֶׁע
	מַאשַׁא
	מַאשֶׁע

296. A female form of *Moshe*. According to Rabbinic authorities, it was created by those who wished to name a girl after her father or grandfather. In this case, the first vowel *a* is fixed and never varies. The family name *Mushin* is derived from this name, the *u* being pronounced like in *nut*.

Matilda — מייטילדה

Old High German.
"Strong one"—"Heroine." Probably a German translation equivalent of Eishet Ḥayyil (A Woman of Valour).

Meita	מֵייטַא
Meite	מֵייטֶע
Meidlin[297]	מֵיידְלִין[297]

297. No connection with Madeline. The ט and the ד are both dentals and hence interchangeable. *Lin* is one of the Old German suffix diminutives. See footnote 135.

Matrona[298] — מאטרונא[298]

French.
"An old woman." Latin: mater—matrona—mother. French:

matrone. One of the amuletic names.

Mata[299]	מַאטַא[299]
Matte	מַאטֶע
Matel	מַאטֶעל
Matil	מַאטִיל
Matela	מַאטֶעלַא
Mateleh	מַאטֶעלֶע

298. An amuletic name akin to *Alte*, *Boba* and *Sabta*.
299. The *rona* ending has been elided followed by the various suffix diminutives.

Mazal[300] מזל[300]

Hebrew. Non-biblical.
"Fortune"—"Good luck." In Hebrew it is exclusively a Sefardi female name. In Spain and Italy, it was also translated to Fortuna. Ashkenazi Jewesses translated it into German—Glück, and finally into Yiddish—Glick, Glickel.

Glück[301]	גלוּק[302, 301]
Glueck[302]	גלִיקל
Glukel	גלוּקֶעל
Glukil	גלוּקִיל
Glick[302]	גלִיק[302]
Glikel	גלִיקל
Gliklen	גלִיקֶעל
	גלִיקִיל
	גלִיקלן

300. Probably an amuletic name. In Hebrew, it is almost exclusively used by Sefardi Jewesses. See footnote 5.
301. The German translation, and hence into Yiddish.
302. Family names derived from these forms. The origins of the family name forms *Gluck(s)man* and *Glick(s)man* are difficult to ascertain. The *man* may be a diminutive suffix, see footnote 36, or the name may simply imply a "man of fortune."

Menuḥah[303, 304] מנוּחה[304, 303]

Hebrew. Non-biblical.
"Peaceful"—"Quite"—"Restful." Feminine form of Mano'aḥ and Menaḥem.

Muna	מוּנַא

Munia	מוניַא
Mune	מונֶע
Munie	מוניֶע
Menia	מֶעניַא
Menie	מֶעניֶע
Mina	מינַא
Minneh	מינֶע
Minka[304a]	[304a]מינקַא
Minke	מינקֶע
Mindel[305, 306]	[306, 305]מינדל
Mindil	מינדֶעל
Mindul	מינדיל
	מינדול

303. The family name *Menuḥin* derives from the original name form. The famous violinist *Yehudi Menuhin* obviously had a female progenitor called *Menuḥah*.
304. Amongst Sefardi Jewry there exists the female name *Consolo*.
304a. The family names *Minkis—Minkes* and *Minkin—Menkin* derive from these forms.
305. See footnote 229.
306. The family name *Mindlin* derives from these diminutive forms.

Miryam (Miriam) מרים

Biblical, Shemot, 15:20.
"Bitter" (in plural form). Sister of Aharon and Moshe. Because she was born to her parents, Amram the Levite and Yokheved, during the period of bitter bondage in Egypt, she was named Miryam.

Mira	מירַא
Mireh	מירֶע
Mirel	מירֶעל
Mirela[307]	[307]מירֶעלַא
Mirele[307]	[307]מירֶעלֶע
Mirka[308]	[308]מירקַא
Mirke	מירקֶע
Merel[309]	[309]מֶערֶעל
Merele	מֶערֶעלֶע
Merka[310]	[310]מֶערקַא
Merke	מֶערקֶע
Merkel[311]	[311]מֶערקֶעל
Mariyam[312]	[312]מַאריאַם

307. The family names *Mireles* and *Mirelis* derive from these forms.
308. The family names *Mirkin*, *Mirkis* and *Mirkes* derive from this form.
309. The family names *Merl* and *Merlin* derive from this form. Not to be confused with the character in old English legends.
310. The family names *Merkes* and *Merkin* derive from this form.
311. The family names *Merkel* and *Merkil* derive from this form.
312. A Slavic variation used by Jewish woman.

Miryam Rachelle (Miriam Rashe)[313] — מרים ראשי[313]

Biblical. Shemot, 15:20, Bereishit, 29:6.
Two Hebrew names: Miryam—Raḥeil. Contracted and diminutised to Mariyasha. In Russian, Miryam is pronounced also—Maryam. A diminutive of the French pronunciation of Raḥeil (Rachelle) is Rashe. Maryam and Rashe contracted to Mariyasha.

Mariyasha[314]	מַרְיַיאשַׁא[314]
Mariyashe	מַרְיַיאשֶׁע
Mariyashel	מַארְיַיאשַׁא
Mariyashil	מַארְיַיאשֶׁע
Mariyashka	מַארְיַיאשֶׁעל
Mariyashke	מַארְיַיאשִׁיל
	מַארְיַיאשְׁקַא
	מַארְיַיאשְׁקֶע

313. See diminutive form of *Rachelle*.
314. See footnote 275.

Muskat[315, 316] — מוּשׁקט[316, 315]

Old French.
"Nutmeg." Muscade.

Muskatel[317]	מוּשְׁקַטל[317]
Mushka	מוּשְׁקַא
Mushke	מוּשְׁקֶע
Muska	מוּסְקַא
Muske	מוּסְקֶע
Meshka	מֶעשְׁקַא
Meshke	מֶעשְׁקֶע

315. Also adopted as a family name.
316. Probably "nutmeg."
317. No direct relation to muscatel, the grape. Muskat plus the Old German

suffix *el* arrives by coincidence at the same phonetics.

Naḥalah — נחלה

Hebrew. Non-biblical.
"Inherited eternal possession."

Nakha[318]	נאַכאַ[318]
Nakhe	נאַכע
Nakhla	נאַכלאַ
Nakhle	נאַכלע
Nakhli	נאַכלי

318. The ח hardened to a כ. See footnote 65.

Neḥamah[319] — נחמה

Hebrew. Non-biblical.
"Comfort"—"Rest from anguish." Feminine form of Naḥum, Neḥemyah and Naḥman.

Nekha	נעכאַ
Nekhe	נעכע
Nekhel	נעכעל
Neḥamka[320]	נְחַמקאַ[320]
Neḥamke	נְחַמקע
Neḥamel	נְחַמעל

319. See footnote 304.
320. The family names *Neḥamkin—Naḥamkin* derive from this form.

Peninah[321] — פנינה[321]

Biblical. Shmueil I, 1:2.
"A pearl." Co-wife of Elkanah. Until her co-wife Ḥannah bore their husband a son, Shmueil the Prophet, she alone bore children. Ḥannah was originally barren.

Nina[322]	נינאַ[322]
Ninneh	נינע
Perel[323]	פּערעל[323]
Perele[323a]	פּערעלע[323a]
Perril	פּעריל

321. See also *Margolah*.

322. No connection with the Italian name of the same spelling.
323. The family name *Perlov—Perlow* derives from this form.
323a. The family names *Perl*, *Perels*, *Pereles* and *Perlin* derive from this form. *Perlman* is also derived from this form. See footnote 36.

Puah[324] פּוּעָה[324]

Biblical. Shemot, 1:15.
"To cry aloud." One of the midwives who were instructed by Pharoah to tell all the Jewish women that they must kill all male babies born to them. Puah was actually Miryam, the older sister of Moshe. She carried this additional name because "she used to gently soothe the babies when they cried."

Pei'ah	פֵּייַאה
Pei'eh	פֵּייֵעה
Pei'al	פֵּייַאל
Pei'el	פֵּייֵעל
Pei'ale	פֵּייַאלֶע
Pei'ele	פֵּייֵעלֶע
Pai'ah	פַּאיַא
Pai'eh	פַּאיֵע
Paika[325]	פַּאיקַא[325]
Paike	פַּאיקֶע

324. A bibical name. See Exodus, 1:15.
325. The family name *Peikowitz—Paikowitz* derives from this form. Another name derivative is *Pikus* (pronounced P*ai*kus).

Raḥeil (Rachel—Rachelle) רחל

Biblical. Bereishit, 29:6.
"A ewe of one year or older." The name suggests tenderness. Younger daughter of Lavan (Laban) the Aramaen, and wife of Yaakov, her first cousin. Mother of Yoseif and Binyamin.

Raḥel	רָאכַא
Roḥel	רָאכֶע
Rokha	רָאכַאלֶע
Rokhe	רָאכֶעלֶע
Rokhale	רָאכלִין[326]
Rokhele	רֶעכַא
Rokhlin[326]	רֶעכֶע
Rekha	רֵייחִיל
Rekhe	רֶעלַא

Reiḥil	רֶעלֶע
Rela	רֶעלִין
Releh	רֵייעֶלִינַא
Relin	רֶעקֶעל[327]
Reiyelina	רִיקל
Rekel[327]	רִיקלַא
Rikel	רִיקלֶע
Rikla	רַאשַא[328]
Rikle	רַאשֶע
Rasha[328]	רַאשִי
Rashe	רַאשֶעל
Rashi	רַאשִיל
Rashel	רַאשקַא[329]
Rashil	רַאשקֶע
Rashka[329]	רִישַא
Rashke	רִישֶע
Risha	רַאסִיַא[330]
Rishe	רַאסִיע
Rasia[330]	רַאסִי
Rasie	רַאסקַא[329]
Rasi	רַאסקֶע
Raska[329]	
Raske	

326. This form became a family name.
327. See footnote 273. However, in this case the ח became a simple *k*.
328. All forms with the שׁ derive from the Old French *Rachelle*.
329. The family names *Raskin* and *Rashkin* derive from these forms.
330. The Lithuanian Yiddish pronunciation often confuses the שׁ and the שׂ.

Rivkah (Rebecca)   רבקה

Biblical. Bereishit, 22:23.
"A woman who takes a man's heart." Rivkah was the daughter of
Betu'eil, son of Naḥor, the brother of Avraham. She was the wife
of Yitzḥak, her first cousin, once removed, and bore him the
twins, Yaakov and Eisav.

Rivke[331]	רִיבקֶע[331]
Rivah	רִיבַה
Riva	רִיבַא
Riveh	רִיבֶע
Rivel	רִיבֶעל
Rivlin[332]	רִיבלִין[332]

Rivkela	רִיבקֶעלַא
Rivkele	רִיבקֶעלֶע

331. The family names *Rivkes*, *Rivkin* and *Rivkind* derive from this form.
332. Also adopted as a family name. One such family has been in Jerusalem since 1804 and is still going strong today.

Roda (Rhoda)[333] — [333]ראדא

Greek.
"A rose."

Rodde	רָאדֶע
Rodel	רוֹדַא
Rodka[334]	רוֹדֶע
Rodke	רָאדֶעל
Reddel[335]	[334]רָאדקַא
	רָאדקֶע
	[335]רֶעדֶעל

333. The word "red" originates from the Greek *rhoda*. Through to Latin, it became *rosa* from whence we have the English *rose* which refers either to the flower or the colour of the rose flower.
334. The family name *Rodkin* and *Rodkevitch* derive from this form.
335. The family name *Redlich* derives from this form.

Roza[336] — [336]רוזא

Latin.
"A rose." Came into Old German and from the German into Yiddish.

Rozeh	רָאזֶע
Roiza	רוֹיזַא
Roizeh[337]	[337]רוֹיזֶע
Reizeh[338]	[338]רֵייזֶע
Reiza[339]	[339]רֵייזַא
Reizel	רֵייזֶעל
Reizil	רֵייזִיל
Rizil	רִיזִיל
Rossa	רָאסַא
Rosseh	רָאסֶע
Rushka[340]	[340]רוּשקַא
Rushke	רוּשקֶע

336. One of the colour group; see footnote 228. The name *Roza* has caused

confusion. Most have presumed that it is a translation of *Shoshanah*. The majority of authorities claim that *Shoshanah* refers to the *lily*, or even flowers in general. In 16th-century Jewish Burial Societies' Registers (Pinkassim), the Yiddish translation of *Shoshanah* has been found to be *Blumah* (Yiddish: flower). Obviously, we refer to the original usage and meanings of these personal female names. After so many centuries, as with many Yiddish names, their original meanings have become lost.

Also, as an independent name, *Roza* meaning *rose* was adopted for use among Jewish women, but originally not as a translation from Hebrew. The form *Roza* is very popular amongst Sefardi women.

337. The family name *Roizes* derives from this form.
338. The family name *Reizes* derives from this form.
339. See footnote 104.
340. See footnote 330.

Ruth[342] — רוּת[342]

Biblical. Ruth, 1:4.

"Friendship"—"Friendly"—"Willing." From the root word *Re'ut*. Ruth, the Moabitess, was the widow of Khilyon son of Elimelekh and Naomi. She became a righteous proselyte to Judaism, and on the death of her husband she returned with her mother-in-law to Beit Leḥem in the Land of Yehudah. She remarried to Boaz, a relative of her dead previous father-in-law Elimelekh. King David descended from this union in the direct male line.

Rus	רוּתל
Rut	רוּתוּל[343]
Rutl	רִיטל
Rutul[343]	רִיטֶעל
Ritl	רִיטלַא
Rittel	רִיטלֶע
Ritla	
Ritleh	

342. Original Hebrew pronounced the ת as *thav*. Many living old-timers amongst Yemenite Jews still pronounce the letter as *thav*. In all forms the *ut* is pronounced like in the English word "put."
343. Sometimes a first vowel sound influences the second and last vowel to be the same.

Sabta[344] — סבתא[344]

Aramaic.

"Grandmother"—"Old woman." One of the female amuletic names. Akin to the Hebrew seiva (old).

Sabatka[345]
Sabatke
Sabatki
Soba
Sob'l
Sobel[346]

סַאבַּטַא
סַאבַּטקַא[345]
סַאבַּטקֶע
סַאבַּטקִי
סָאבַּא
סָאבּל
סָאבֶּעל[346]

344. An amuletic name similar to the Yiddish *Boba*. See also footnote 5.
345. All these spelling variations became a family name. The family originated in Prague. The first-known progenitor with this name was Rabbi Tzvi Hirsch *Sabatka*, son-in-law of the renowned MaHaRal of Prague, Rabbi *Yehudah Liwa* (Old Judeo-German for the later Yiddish form, *Leibe*). This author descends from this Rabbi Tzvi Hirsch *Sabatka* and his wife *Tilla*, daughter of the MaHaRal.
346. The family name *Sobel* probably derives from this form. It is possible, however, that the family name *Sobel* derives from the German word for the fur, sable, denoting a dealer in furs.

Salida[347] זעלדה

Old German.
"Happiness." Probably a feminine variation translation of Asher.

Zelda
Zelde

זֶעלדַא
זֶעלדֶע

347. Perhaps a female equivalent for *Asher* (happy).

Sarah שׂרה

Biblical. Bereishit, 11:29, 17:15.
"Ruler"—"Chieftainess"—"Princess." Sarah was a niece of her husband Avraham. She was the mother of Yitzḥak and the sister of Lot. Her original name was *Sarai*—my princess (in a limited manner). The Almighty changed the י in her name to a ה inferring a princess in the general sense. The ה is the key letter of the Almighty's name. Sarah was the progenitress of the Jewish People.

Sorah
Sorrel
Sorril

סָארֶעל
סָארִיל
סָארקַא

Sorka	סאָרקע
Sorke	סאָרקעל
Sorkel	סאָרקיל
Sorkil	[348]סערעל
Serrel[348]	סעריל
Serril	סירעל
Sirrel	סיריל
Sirril	[349]סירקא
Sirka[349]	סירקע
Sirke	סירקי
Sirki	

348. The family name *Serlin* derives from these forms.
349. The family names *Sirkes* and *Sirkin* derive from these forms. See also footnote 374.

Shoshanah[350] — [350]שושנה

Hebrew. Non-biblical.
"A lily." Also, the name was used for flowers in general.

Shushanah	שושא
Shosha	שושע
Shoshe	שושעל
Shoshel	שושקא
Shoshka	שושקע
Shoshke	[352, 351, 350]בלומא
Bluma[350, 351, 352]	בלומע
Blumeh	בלומעל
Blumel	בלומקא
Blumka	בלומקע
Blumke	בלימא
Blima	בלימע
Blime	בלימעל
Blimel	

350. See footnote 336.
351. Yiddish for flower.
352. The family name *Blum* (*Bloom*) derives from these forms.

Shulamit (Shulamis) — שולמית

Hebrew. Non-biblical.
The biblical meaning is Shulamitess—a woman from Shuleim.

However, it was adopted at a later period as a feminine equivalent of Shlomoh.

Shula	שׁוּלַא
Shuleh	שׁוּלֶע
Shulka[353]	שׁוּלְקַא[353]
Shulke	שׁוּלְקֶע

353. The family name *Shulkin* derives from these forms.

Simḥah[354] שׂמחה[354]

Hebrew. Non-biblical.
"Joy"—"Rejoice at heart"—"Spiritual joy." Originally both a male and female name.

Sima	שִׂימַא
Simmeh	שִׂימֶע
Simka[355, 356]	סִימַא
Simkeh	שִׂימֶע
	שִׂימְקַא[356, 355]
	שִׂימְקֶע
	סִימְקַא
	סִימְקֶע

354. *Simḥah* was originally both a male and female name. Today, the name amongst Ashkenazi Jews is almost absolutely a male one. The diminutive forms, however, have remained amongst Ashkenazi Jews completely as female names. Amongst Sefardi Jews, however, the original *Simḥah* has remained a female name, also.
355. The family name *Simkin* is derived from these forms.
356. The כ has interchanged with ח and is not the Slavic diminutive suffix of *ka* or *ke*. See footnote 273.

Tamar תמר

Biblical. Bereishit, 38:6.
"Palm tree"—"Date." Wife of Eir, first born of Yehudah. Tamar is a masculine form of the word. Tamarah is the feminine form of the word. The form Tamarah as a name is non-biblical.

Tamarah	תַּמַרַה
Temer	טֶעמֶער
Temerel	טֶעמֶערֶעל
Temeril	טֶעמֶערִיל
Temma	טֶעמַא

Temmeh — טעמע
Temel — טעמעל
Temka[357] — טעמקא[357]
Temke — טעמקע
Tamarka[358] — טאמארקא[358]
Tamarke — טאמארקע

357. The family name *Temkin* derives from these forms.
358. The family names *Tamarkin* and *Tumarkin* derive from these forms.

Tehillah — תהלה

Hebrew. Non-biblical.
"Praise"—"Noble light"—"Majestic glory." From the root word Halleil (Halleiluyah—Praise the Lord.)

Tilla[359] — טילא[359]
Tilleh[359, 360] — טילע[360, 359]
Tilka[361] — טילקא[361]
Tilkeh — טילקע

359. The soft ה has been elided. See footnotes 1 and 345.
360. The family name *Tilles* (*Tillis*) derives from this form.
361. The family name *Tilkin* derives from this form.

Tikvah[362] — תקוה[362]

Non-biblical and biblical. Melakhim II, 22:14.
"Hope." Outside of biblical use, it is exclusively a female name. In the biblical source, he was the father of Shulam, the husband of Ḥuldah the Prophetess.

Shprintza — שפרינצא
Shprintze — שפרינצע
Shprintzel — שפרינצעל
Shprintzak[363] — שפרינצאק[363]
Shprintzik — שפרינציק

362. The name *Tikvah* is a popular Israeli female name, but there is no evidence that the Hebrew form was ever used in pre-expulsion Spain. It seems that the silent feelings of the Jews at that time were expressed in the local tongue and that the original name was indeed reduced to *Shprintza*. It was very popular among East European Jewesses.
363. The family name *Shprintzak* derives from these forms.

Tirtzah תִּרצָה

Biblical. Bamidbar, 26:33.
"A young deer." One of the daughters of Tzelafḥad. Feminine gender of the root word ratz (to run).

Tirtze[363a]	טִירצַא
Tirtzel	טִירצֶע[363a]
	טִירצֶל
	טִירצֶיל
	תִּרצֶל
	תִּרצֶעל

363a. *Tirtzeh* with the *e* vowel is masculine. In this case it is simply the Yiddish phonetical pronunciation, and not a grammatical form.

Tovah טוֹבָה

Hebrew. Non-biblical.
"A good woman." Probably the equivalent of the male name Toviyah.

Tovel	טוֹבל
Gutte[364]	גוּטֶע[364]
Gutta	גוּטַא
Guttel	גוּטֶעל
Guttil	גוּטִיל
Gitta[365]	גִיטַא[365]
Gitte	גִיטֶע
Gittel	גִיטֶעל
Gittil	גִיטִיל
Dobra[366]	דָאברַא[366]
Dobreh	דָאברֶע
Dobril	דָאבּרִיל
Dobrish[366a]	דָאבּרִיש[366a]
Dobrush	דָאברוּש
Dobrushka[367]	דָאברוּשקַא[367]
Dobrushke	דָאברוּשקֶע

364. From the German translation *Güte*.
365. The transformation of the vowel *u* into an *i* occurs repeatedly in the different colloquial dialectic phonetics of Yiddish. See also *Buna—Bina*.
366. The Slavic translation.
366a. See footnote 1c.

367. The family name *Dobrushkin* derives from these forms. See first statement of footnote 238.

Tzipporah — צִפּוֹרה

Biblical. Shemot, 2:21.
"A female bird." Daughter of Yitro, the priest of Midyan, who gave her to Moshe as his wife. She bore two sons to Moshe, Geirshom and Eliezer.

Tzippa[368]	צִיפַּא[368]
Tzippe	צִיפֶּע
Tzipka[369]	צִיפְּקַא[369]
Tzipke	צִיפְּקֶע
Foigel[370, 371]	פוֹיקֶעל[371, 370]
Foiglin	פוֹיגלִין
Feiga[372]	פֵּייגַא[372]
Feige	פֵּייגֶע
Feigel	פֵּייגֶעל
Feigele	פֵּייגֶעלֶע
Feigil	פֵּייגִיל
Feiglin[372a]	פֵּייגלִין[372a]

368. The family name *Tzippin* derives from these forms.
369. The family name *Tzipkin* derives from these forms.
370. The original German translation *Vogel*. The *v* is pronounced as an *f* as both letters belong to the labio-dental group.
371. *Vogel* and *Fogel* are popular family names derived from these forms.
372. The family name *Feigin* derives from these.
372a. The family name *Feiglin* derives from this. See footnote 135.

Tzirre[373] — צִירע[373]

Old German.
"Decoration"—"Jewel" To bedeck with jewellry. Zieren.

Tzira	צִירַא
Tzireh	צִירֶע
Tzirel	צִירֶעל
Tzirele	צִירֶעלֶע
Tziril	צִירִיל
Tzirka[374]	צִירקַא[374]
Tzirke	צִירקֶע

373. The Hebrew word to paint, draw or decorate is *le'tzayyer*. The root of

the word is *tzir*. It is possibly a Yiddish adoption that arrived at the name *Tzirre* (a decoration), hence the word for jewel.

374. The family names *Tzirkin* and *Tzirkind* derive from these forms. They were Anglicised to *Zirkin* and *Zirkind*. See also footnote 349. These derivative family names are often confused.

Tzitta צִיטָא

Italian.
"Fast one"—"Energetic." Probably referring to the Eishet Ḥayyil (Woman of Valour).

Tzitte	צִיטֶע
Tzittel	צִיטֶעל
Tzittil	צִיטִיל
Tzeitta[375]	צֵייטָא[375]
Tzeitte	צֵייטֶע
Tzeittel	צֵייטֶעל
Tzeittil	צֵייטִיל
Tzeitlin[376]	צֵייטלִין[376]
Sitta	סִיטָא
Sitte	סִיטֶע
Sittel	סִיטֶעל
Sittil	סִיטִיל

375. The *ei* vowel became the dominant sound in this name even though an occasional *Sitta* turns up.

376. The well-known family name *Tzeitlin (Zeitlin)* is derived from this diminutive form. See footnote 135.

Tzviah צביה

Biblical. Melakhim II, 12:2.
"Female deer"—"Hind"—"Doe." Wife of Aḥazyah, King of Yehudah, and mother of Yeho'ash. She was from Be'eir Sheva.

Tziviah[377]	צִבְיָה[377]
Hinda	הִינדָא
Hinde[378]	הִינדֶע[378]
Hindel[379]	הִינדֶעל[379]
Hindil	הִינדִיל
Hendel[379a]	הֶענדֶעל[379a]
Hendil	הֶענדִיל

377. Both *Tzviah* and *Tziviah* are correct Hebrew pronunciations.

378. Old German translation. Same as "hind" in English.
379. See footnote 65.
379a. Could be an alternative origin of the family name *Hendel*. See footnote 65. The family name *Gendel* may be a Russified version of *Hendel*. See footnote 152.

Yaffah[380] יפה[380]

Hebrew. Non-biblical.
"Beautiful woman." Feminine equivalent of the male name Yefet. Yefet (Japeth) was a son of Noaḥ.

Yaffeh
Sheina[381]
Sheine
Sheindel[382, 383]
Sheindele
Sheindil

יַאפֶא
יַאפֶע
שֵׁיינָא[381]
שֵׁיינֶע
שֵׁיינְדֶעל[383, 382]
שֵׁיינְדֶעלֶע
שֵׁיינְדִיל

380. An ancient and well-established family name. The forms in non-Hebrew languages vary, i.e. *Yoffa*, *Yoffe*, *Yaffe*, *Joffa*, *Joffe*, and also *Yoffin* and *Yaffin*.
381. The family name *Scheiner (Schöner)* derives from this form.
382. See footnote 229.
383. The family names *Schindel*, *Schindler* and *Schindling* derive from these forms.

Yehudit (Judith)[384] יהודית[384]

Biblical. Bereishit, 26:34.
"To thank (God)." Feminine form of Yehudah. Daughter of Be'eiri the Hittite, and wife of Eisav.

Also, a non-canonical Second Temple period historical narrative named after the Jewish heroine of the events it describes. When he was in a drunken sleep, she killed Holofornes, chief of the Assyrians who were besieging the Jews. Deprived of their commander-in-chief by Yehudit's courageous deed, the panic-stricken Assyrian soldiers took to their heels.

Yehudis
Yudit[385]
Yudit'l
Yutta[386]

יוּדִית[385]
יוּדִיתְל
יוּטָא
יוּטֶע[386]

Yutte	יוטֶעל
Yuttel	יוטֶעלֶע
Yuttele	ייטַא
Yitta	ייטֶע
Yitte	ייטֶעל
Yittel	אִידִית
Idit	אִיטַא
Itta[387]	אִיטֶע[387]
Itte	אִיטקַא
Itka	אִיטקֶע
Itke	

384. Female form of *Yehudah (Judah)*.
385. In the diminutive forms the ה has been completely elided.
386. Regarding the change from ד to ט, see footnote 29.
387. See footnote 247.

Yiskah[388] (Iscah) (Jessica) יסכה[388]

Biblical. Bereishit, 11:29.
"To see prophetically"—"Sight of royalty"—"Desirous to the eyes."

Yiskoh	אִיסקַא
Iska[389, 390]	אִיסקֶע[390, 389]
Iske	עֶסקַא
Eska[390]	עֶסקֶע[390]
Eske	עֶשקַא
Eshka	עֶשקֶע
Eshke	

388. Another name of *Sarah* our matriarch. See Genesis, 11:29.
389. This is another example of identical diminutive name forms deriving from two different original names. In this case, *Eska—Eske* are basically the root of the name form, but with the name *Esther*, *Eska—Eske* are pure diminutive forms. See footnote 246.
390. See last comment of footnote 247.

Yoḥanah[391] יוחנה[391]

Hebrew. Non-biblical.
"She is graced." Feminine form of Yoḥanan.

Yakhna[392]	יַאחנַא[392]
Yakhne	יַאחנֶע

יַאכנַא
יַאכנֶע

391. Female form of *Yoḥanan*.
392. See footnote 259.

Yokheved (Jochobed) יוכבד

Biblical. Shemot, 6:20.
"Honour of God." Contraction of the two Hebrew words: Yoh—Kavod. Yokheved was of the house of Leivi and the wife of Amram. Mother of Miryam, Aharon and Moshe.

Yokha[393]	יוֹכַא[393]
Yokhe	יוֹכֶע
Yakhe	יַאכֶע

393. See footnote 259.

Yonah[394] (Jonah) יוֹנה[394]

Biblical. Melakhim II, 14:25, and the Book of Yonah.
"A dove." In the Hebrew form this is mostly a male name. A Prophet of God whose message was to the Gentile population of Nineveh. Swallowed by and spewed up by a giant whale on refusal to accept the mission the Almighty had sent him on. After his ordeal with the giant whale, he accepted his mission and carried it out.

Yoina[395]	יוֹנַא[395]
Yoino	יוֹנָא
Yoine	יוֹנֶע
Yeina[395]	יֵינַא[395]
Yeino	יֵינָא
Yeine	יֵינֶע
Toiba[395]	טוֹיבַא[395]
Toibe	טוֹיבֶע
Teiba	טֵייבַא[395]
Teibe	טֵייבֶע
Teib'l	טֵייבל
Teibel[394]	טֵייבֶעל[394]
Teibil[394]	טֵייבִיל[394]

394. In the Hebrew form this is mostly a male name. The Yiddish translation form is exclusively a female name. Not to be confused with the male names *Tevel*, a diminutive of *David*, and *Toviyah*. See footnote 30.

395. See footnote 104.

Zissa[396] זיסא[396]

Yiddish.
"Sweet one"—"Sweetie." From the German Züss.

Zisse זִיסֶע[397]
Zissel[397] זִיסֶעל
Zissil זִיסִיל

396. As the Yiddish word for *sweet* has no gender, it was inevitable that the diminutive dynamics made some forms identical for the male and female names. See *Zussman* and footnote 208.
397. The family name *Zislin* is derived from these forms.

BIBLIOGRAPHY

Hebrew

Alfasi, Yitzḥak. *Ha-Ḥasidut*. Tel Aviv: 1974.
Arazy, Dr. Avraham. *Ve-Eileh Sheimot Bnei Yisrael*. (*The Personal Names of the Jews and the Israelis*) Bnei Brak: 1982.
Beilinson, Rabbi Moshe Eliezer. *Shelumei Emunei Yisrael*. Yalkut Mishpaḥot. Odessa: 1898.
Berman, Shlomoh & Mikhal Rabinowitz. *Mishpaḥot K.K. Shklov*. Kovetz Al Yad, Ḥevrat "Mekitzei Nirdamim". New Series, Book I (XI), Jerusalem: 1936.
Brisk, Asher Leib. *Ḥelkat Meḥokek*. Jerusalem: 1895–.
Eisenstadt, Yisrael Tuvia. *Da'at Kedoshim*. St. Petersburg: 1897–98.
Greijewski, Pinḥas ben Tzvi. *Avnei Zikharon*. Vols. 1–15. Jerusalem: 1931–1932.
Gumpertz, Dr. Yeḥiel Gedalyahu. *Kriyat Sheimot Beyisrael*. Tarbiz. Quarterly for Jewish Sciences. 25th year, 1956. J. L. Magnes Press, Hebrew University, Jerusalem.
Heilprin, Rabbi Yeḥiel ben Shlomoh. *Seider Hadorot*. Reprint, Jerusalem: 1956.
Hock, Simon. *Mishpaḥot K.K. Prag* (*Die Familien Prags*). Pressburg: 1892.
Kroll, Zwi & Zadok Leinman. *Beit Ha'Kvarot Hayashan B'Tel Aviv*. Tel Aviv: 1940.
Lawaut, Avraham David ben Yehudah Leib. *Kav Naki*. 3rd. edition (with additions). Otzar Ha-Ḥassidim, Kefar Ḥabad, Israel: 1976.
Levinstein, Rabbi Yosef. *Dor V'Dor V'Dorshov*. Nezaḥ, Tel Aviv: 1949.
Liberman, Yosef. *Shalshelet Ha-Yuḥsin*. Jerusalem: 1978.
Rappaport, Rabbi Shelomoh Yehudah Kohan. *Gal Eid*. Prague: 1856.
Schwartz, Rabbi Pinḥas Zelig. *Sheim Hagedolim Mei'Eretz Hagar*. Revised edition. New York: 1958.
Steinberg, Yehoshua. *Milon Ha-Tenakh*, Ivrit Aramaic. Published by Yizr'el. Tel Aviv: 1960.
Stern, Rabbi Avraham. *Melitzei Eish*. Jerusalem: 1975.
Weinreich, Max. "Bnei Het U'Bnei Ḥet B'Ashkenaz". *Leshoneinu* Vol. 23. The Academy for the Hebrew Language. Jerusalem: 1959.
———. *Tenakh* (Torah - Nevi'im, Ketuvim).
———. *The Babylonian Talmud*.
———. Pinkassim. (Ledgers) of all four Jerusalem Ashkenazi Ḥevrot Kadisha (Burial Societies).
———. Tombstone Inscriptions on the Mount of Olives Cemetery in Jerusalem.

English

Chelminsky-Lajmer, Enrique. *Names, Journal of the American Name Society*. Vol. 23, No. 1. The State University College, Potsdam, New York: March 1975.

Gorr, Rabbi Shmuel. *The Official Gazette* 1921–1948. (Compiled and edited by) Public Announcement of Legal Changes of Names during the British Mandate in Palestine. The Jerusalem Research Institute for Jewish Genealogy and Data Universal Corp. Teaneck, New Jersey, U.S., 1983.

Hyamson, Albert M. "Jewish Surnames." A paper read before the Jewish Social and Literary Society, (London), April 1903. (Reprinted from the *Jewish Literary Annual*).

Kaganoff, Benzion C. *A Dictionary of Jewish Names and Their History*. Schoken Books, New York: 1977.

Rosenberg, Meir. *The Jewish Cat Book...A Different Breed*. (Edited by) Michah Publications, Marblehead, Massachusetts.

Shilstone, Eustace M. *Jewish Monumental Inscriptions in Barbados*. New York, 1956.

Webster, Noah. *New Revised Edition Webster's Daily Use Dictionary*. Grosset & Dunlap, Inc. U.S.: 1938.

———. *Hebrew Bible—English Translation*. Hebrew Publishing Company, New York.

———. Dénombrement des Juifs D'Alsace 1784. (*The Census of the Jews of Alsace in 1784*).

Index to Personal Names

Name	Root Name	Sex
Abba	Avraham	m
Abbale	Avraham	m
Abbele	Avraham	m
Abish	Avraham	m
Abrasha	Avraham	m
Abrashe	Avraham	m
Abrashka	Avraham	m
Abrashke	Avraham	m
Abush	Avraham	m
Adel	Adinah	f
Adela	Adinah	f
Adinah	Adinah	f
Aharon	Aharon	m
Aizik	Yitzhak	m
Aizikel	Yitzhak	m
Aizikman	Yitzhak	m
Aizlin	Yitzhak	m
Aizman	Yitzhak	m
Aleksander	Aleksander	m
Aleksender	Aleksander	m
Aliksender	Aleksander	m
Alta	Alte	f
Alte	Alte	f
Alter	Alter	m
Altir	Alter	m
Altmann	Alter	m
Amalya	Amelia	f
Amalye	Amelia	f
Amelia	Amelia	f
Anschel	Asher	m
Anschil	Asher	m
Anselm	Asher	m
Anshel	Asher	m
Anshil	Asher	m
Anzel	Asher	m
Anzil	Asher	m
Arel	Aharon	m
Arel	Aryeh	m
Arele	Aharon	m
Ari'	Aryeh	m
Arik Artze	Aryeh	m
Arke	Aryeh	m
Arke	Aharon	m
Aron	Aharon	m
Artzi	Aryeh	m
Arush	Aharon	m
Arushka	Aharon	m
Arushke	Aharon	m
Aryeh	Aryeh	m
Asher	Asher	m
Asher'l	Asher	m
Asherel	Asher	m
Asna	Asnat	f
Asnas	Asnat	f
Asnat	Asnat	f
Asne	Asnat	f
Asnes	Asnat	f
Avigaiyil	Avigaiyil	f
Avigal	Avigaiyil	f
Avigali	Avigaiyil	f
Avraham	Avraham	m
Avram	Avraham	m
Avrel	Avraham	m
Avremel	Avraham	m
Avremele	Avraham	m
Avremka	Avraham	m
Avremke	Avraham	m
Avril	Avraham	m
Avrom	Avraham	m
Barka	Batyah	f
Barukh	Barukh	m
Basel	Batyah	f
Basha	Batyah	f
Bashala	Batyah	f
Bashale	Batyah	f
Basharel	Batyah	f
Bashe	Batyah	f
Basya	Batyah	f
Basye	Batyah	f
Batka	Batyah	f
Batke	Batyah	f
Batyah	Batyah	f
Beila	Bilhah	f
Beilah	Bilhah	f
Beile	Bilhah	f
Beilka	Bilhah	f
Beilke	Bilhah	f
Beinis	Benyamin	m
Beinish	Benyamin	m
Beinush	Benyamin	m
Beirakh	Berekhiah	m
Beirekh	Berekhiah	m
Beirikh	Berekhiah	m
Benchel	Bentzion	m
Benchil	Bentzion	m
Bendet	Barukh	m
Bendet'l	Barukh	m
Bendit	Barukh	m

Name	Root Name	Sex
Bentche	Bentzion	m
Bentze	Bentzion	m
Bentzel	Bentzion	m
Bentzil	Bentzion	m
Bentzion	Bentzion	m
Benyamin	Benyamin	m
Benyomin	Benyamin	m
Ber	Dov	m
Bere	Dov	m
Berek	Dov	m
Berekhiah	Berekhiah	m
Berel	Dov	m
Berele	Dov	m
Berelein	Dov	m
Berelin	Dov	m
Berik	Dov	m
Berish	Dov	m
Berke	Dov	m
Berko	Dov	m
Berlein	Dov	m
Berlin	Dov	m
Berman	Dov	m
Berush	Dov	m
Besel	Batyah	f
Beserel	Batyah	f
Betzalel	Betzalel	m
Bilah	Bilhah	f
Bileh	Bilhah	f
Bilhah	Bilhah	f
Billa	Bilhah	f
Bille	Bilhah	f
Bina	Bunah	f
Bineh	Bunah	f
Binem	Bunim	m
Binim	Bunim	m
Binis	Benyamin	m
Birakh	Berekhiah	m
Birekh	Berekhiah	m
Blima	Shoshanah	f
Blime	Shoshanah	f
Blimel	Shoshanah	f
Bluma	Shoshanah	f
Blumeh	Shoshanah	f
Blumel	Shoshanah	f
Blumka	Shoshanah	f
Blumke	Shoshanah	f
Boba	Boba	f
Bobala	Boba	f
Bobale	Boba	f
Bobe	Boba	f
Bobela	Boba	f
Bobele	Boba	f

Name	Root Name	Sex
Bobinczka	Boba	f
Bobinczke	Boba	f
Bodana	Bodhana	f
Bodane	Bodhana	f
Bodhana	Bodhana	f
Bodhane	Bodhana	f
Bodna	Bodhana	f
Bodne	Bodhana	f
Bodnia	Bodhana	f
Bodnie	Bodhana	f
Bonem	Bunim	m
Bonim	Bunim	m
Borukh	Barukh	m
Breina	Breina	f
Breindel	Breina	f
Breindil	Breina	f
Breine	Breina	f
Broina	Breina	f
Broindel	Breina	f
Broindil	Breina	f
Broine	Breina	f
Bruna	Breina	f
Brundel	Breina	f
Brundil	Breina	f
Brune	Breina	f
Bubuna	Bunah	f
Buna	Bunah	f
Bunah	Bunah	f
Bunalah	Bunah	f
Bunale	Bunah	f
Bunczeka	Bunah	f
Bunczeke	Bunah	f
Bundel	Bunah	f
Buneh	Bunah	f
Bunem	Bunim	m
Bunim	Bunim	m
Bunina	Bunah	f
Buninne	Bunah	f
Bunya	Bunah	f
Bunye	Bunah	f
Cule	Yakov	m
Culi	Yakov	m
Czarna	Czarna	f
Czarne	Czarna	f
Czarni	Czarna	f
Dan	Daniel	m
Dan'l	Daniel	m
Dani	Daniel	m
Daniel	Daniel	m
David	David	m
Denel	Daniel	m
Devel	David	m

Name	Root Name	Sex
Devorah	Devorah	f
Devvil	David	m
Didya	Gottlieb	m
Didye	Gottlieb	m
Doba	Dobah	f
Dobah	Dobah	f
Dobe	Dobah	f
Dobka	Dobah	f
Dobke	Dobah	f
Dobra	Tovah	f
Dobreh	Tovah	f
Dobril	Tovah	f
Dobrish	Tovah	f
Dobrush	Tovah	f
Dobrusha	Tovah	f
Dov	Dov	m
Dover	Dov	m
Dovid	David	m
Dovid'l	David	m
Dovidka	David	m
Dovidke	David	m
Dreiza	Drozha	f
Dreize	Drozha	f
Dreizel	Drozha	f
Dreizil	Drozha	f
Drezel	Drozha	f
Drezil	Drozha	f
Drozha	Drozha	f
Drozhe	Drozha	f
Drozna	Drozha	f
Drozne	Drozha	f
Duber	Dov	m
Dveira	Devorah	f
Dveire	Devorah	f
Dvoira	Devorah	f
Dvoirale	Devorah	f
Dvoire	Devorah	f
Dvoirel	Devorah	f
Dvoirele	Devorah	f
Dvoirka	Devorah	f
Dvoirke	Devorah	f
Dvosha	Devorah	f
Dvoshe	Devorah	f
Dvoshel	Devorah	f
Dvoshka	Devorah	f
Dvoshke	Devorah	f
Ednah	Adinah	f
Efraiyim	Efraiyim	m
Efroika	Efraiyim	m
Efroike	Efraiyim	m
Efroimel	Efraiyim	m
Efroimka	Efraiyim	m

Name	Root Name	Sex
Efroimke	Efraiyim	m
Efrom	Efraiyim	m
Eida	Adinah	f
Eide	Adinah	f
Eidel	Adinah	f
Eidela	Adinah	f
Eidele	Adinah	f
Eidil	Adinah	f
Eidul	Adinah	f
Einikh	Ḥanokh	m
Eiver	Eiver	m
Eiverman	Eiver	m
Eivril	Eiver	m
Eivril	Avraham	m
Elḥanan	Elḥanan	m
Elazar	Elazar	m
Eli	Eliyahu	m
Eliezer	Eliezer	m
Elik	Eliyahu	m
Elimelekh	Elimelekh	m
Elinka	Eliyahu	m
Elinke	Eliyahu	m
Eliyahu	Eliyahu	m
Eliyohu	Eliyahu	m
Elka	Illa	f
Elke	Illa	f
Ella	Illa	f
Elleh	Illa	f
Ellush	Illa	f
Elḥonon	Elḥanan	m
Elozer	Elazar	m
Elozor	Elazar	m
Elya	Eliyahu	m
Elyakim	Elyakim	m
Elyakum	Elyakim	m
Elye	Eliyahu	m
Elyokim	Elyakim	m
Elyokum	Elyakim	m
Emanuel	Emanuel	m
Emeline	Amelia	f
Enikh	Ḥanokh	m
Enzel	Asher	m
Enzil	Asher	m
Enzlin	Asher	m
Eshka	Yiskah	f
Eshke	Yiskah	f
Eska	Ester	f
Eska	Yiskah	f
Eske	Ester	f
Eske	Yiskah	f
Esriel	Gotthelf	m
Essa	Ester	f

Name	Root Name	Sex
Esse	Ester	f
Ester	Ester	f
Esterel	Ester	f
Esteril	Ester	f
Estrina	Ester	f
Etka	Ester	f
Etke	Ester	f
Etta	Ester	f
Ette	Ester	f
Ettel	Ester	f
Ettil	Ester	f
Evril	Efraiyim	m
Ezriel	Gotthelf	m
Feiga	Tzipporah	f
Feige	Tzipporah	f
Feigel	Tzipporah	f
Feigele	Tzipporah	f
Feigil	Tzipporah	f
Feiglin	Tzipporah	f
Feish	Efraiyim	m
Feishel	Efraiyim	m
Feishil	Efraiyim	m
Feitel	Ḥayyim	m
Feivel	Shraga Feivush	m
Feivil	Shraga Feivush	m
Feivish	Shraga Feivush	m
Feivul	Shraga Feivush	m
Fish	Efraiyim	m
Fishel	Efraiyim	m
Fishil	Efraiyim	m
Foigel	Tzipporah	f
Foiglin	Tzipporah	f
Fol	Rafael	m
Folk	Rafael	m
Folka	Rafael	m
Folke	Rafael	m
Folle	Rafael	m
Follik	Rafael	m
Frada	Frieda	f
Frade	Frieda	f
Fradel	Frieda	f
Fradil	Frieda	f
Fradka	Frieda	f
Fradke	Frieda	f
Freida	Frieda	f
Freide	Frieda	f
Freidel	Frieda	f
Freidil	Frieda	f
Freidka	Frieda	f
Freidke	Frieda	f
Frieda	Frieda	f
Friede	Frieda	f

Name	Root Name	Sex
Friedel	Frieda	f
Friedil	Frieda	f
Friedka	Frieda	f
Friedke	Frieda	f
Froim	Efraiyim	m
Froimel	Efraiyim	m
Froimka	Efraiyim	m
Froimke	Efraiyim	m
Froma	Frommet	f
Fromme	Frommet	f
Frommel	Frommet	f
Frommet	Frommet	f
Frommetel	Frommet	f
Fruma	Frommet	f
Frumka	Frommet	f
Frumke	Frommet	f
Frumme	Frommet	f
Frummel	Frommet	f
Frummet	Frommet	f
Frummetel	Frommet	f
Galleh	Gelleh	f
Galyah	Gelleh	f
Gedalyah	Gedalyah	f
Gellah	Gelleh	f
Gelleh	Gelleh	f
Genana	Genana	f
Genaneh	Genana	f
Genena	Genana	f
Genendel	Genana	f
Genendil	Genana	f
Genenneh	Genana	f
Gentelle	Gentille	f
Gentila	Gentille	f
Gentille	Gentille	f
Gershel	Tzvi	m
Getz	Gottschalk	m
Getzel	Gottschalk	m
Ginesha	Genana	f
Gineshe	Genana	f
Gisha	Gisse	f
Gishe	Gisse	f
Gissa	Gisse	f
Gisse	Gisse	f
Gissel	Gisse	f
Gissela	Gisse	f
Gissele	Gisse	f
Gitta	Tovah	f
Gitte	Tovah	f
Gittel	Tovah	f
Gittil	Tovah	f
Gizza	Gisse	f
Gizze	Gisse	f

Name	Root Name	Sex
Glick	Mazal	f
Glikel	Mazal	f
Gliklen	Mazal	f
Gluck	Mazal	f
Glueck	Mazal	f
Glukel	Mazal	f
Glukil	Mazal	f
Godel	Gedalyah	m
Godil	Gedalyah	m
Godul	Gedalyah	m
Goetz	Gottschalk	m
Golda	Golda	f
Goldeh	Golda	f
Goldeleh	Golda	f
Goldinchke	Golda	f
Gotsch	Gottschalk	m
Gotsh'l	Gottschalk	m
Gotthelf	Gotthelf	m
Gottlieb	Gottlieb	m
Gottschalk	Gottschalk	m
Grina	Gruna	f
Grineh	Gruna	f
Gruna	Gruna	f
Grune	Gruna	f
Grunia	Gruna	f
Grunie	Gruna	f
Gulka	Yakov	m
Gulke	Yakov	m
Gulko	Yakov	m
Gutta	Tovah	f
Gutte	Tovah	f
Guttel	Tovah	f
Guttil	Tovah	f
Hadas	Hadassah	f
Hadassah	Hadassah	f
Hades	Hadassah	f
Hallah	Gelleh	f
Halleh	Gelleh	f
Hana	Ḥannah	f
Hasha	Ketziah	f
Hasheh	Ketziah	f
Haska	Ketziah	f
Haskeh	Ketziah	f
Hassia	Ketziah	f
Hassieh	Ketziah	f
Heiman	Ḥayyim	m
Heinikh	Ḥanokh	m
Heishe	Yehoshua	m
Heishek	Yehoshua	m
Heishel	Yehoshua	m
Heishik	Yehoshua	m
Hellah	Gelleh	f
Helleh	Gelleh	f
Hendel	Hanokh	m
Hendel	Tzviah	f
Hendil	Hanokh	m
Hendil	Tzviah	f
Hendl	Hanokh	m
Henel	Hanokh	m
Henikh	Hanokh	m
Henli	Hanokh	m
Henna	Hannah	f
Henne	Hannah	f
Henya	Hannah	f
Henye	Hannah	f
Henzel	Asher	m
Henzil	Asher	m
Hersch	Tzvi	m
Herschel	Tzvi	m
Herschil	Tzvi	m
Hertz	Tzvi	m
Hertzel	Tzvi	m
Hertzke	Tzvi	m
Hertzl	Tzvi	m
Heshe	Yehoshua	m
Heshel	Yehoshua	m
Heshke	Yehoshua	m
Hess	Ḥizkiyahu	m
Hessel	Yehoshua	m
Hessil	Yehoshua	m
Heyman	Ḥayyim	m
Hezkel	Yehezkiel	m
Hinda	Tzviah	f
Hinde	Tzviah	f
Hindel	Tzviah	f
Hindil	Tzviah	f
Hirsch	Tzvi	m
Hirschel	Tzvi	m
Hirtz	Tzvi	m
Hiz	Ḥizkiyahu	m
Hoda	Hadassah	f
Hodas	Hadassah	f
Hoddeh	Hadassah	f
Hodel	Hadassah	f
Hodes	Hadassah	f
Hodiah	Hadassah	f
Hodil	Hadassah	f
Ḥacze	Yeḥezkiel	m
Ḥai	Ḥayyim	m
Ḥaikel	Ḥayyim	m
Ḥaiman	Ḥayyim	m
Ḥaiyah Henne	Ḥaiyah Henne	f
Ḥaiyala	Ḥaiyyah	f
Ḥaiyalle	Ḥaiyyah	f

Name	Root Name	Sex
Ḥaiyenna	Ḥaiyah Henne	f
Ḥaiyenneh	Ḥaiyah Henne	f
Ḥaiyetta	Ḥaiyyah Esther	f
Ḥaiyetteh	Ḥaiyyah Esther	f
Ḥaiyyah	Ḥaiyyah	f
Ḥaiyyah Esther	Ḥaiyyah Esther	f
Ḥanala	Ḥannah	f
Ḥanalle	Ḥannah	f
Ḥanan	Yoḥanan	m
Ḥanan	Elḥanan	m
Ḥancze	Ḥannah	f
Ḥanela	Ḥannah	f
Ḥanelle	Ḥannah	f
Ḥaniczka	Ḥannah	f
Ḥaniczke	Ḥannah	f
Ḥanna	Ḥannah	f
Ḥannah	Ḥannah	f
Ḥanne	Ḥannah	f
Ḥanokh	Ḥanokh	m
Ḥaskel	Yeḥezkiel	m
Ḥatzkel	Yeḥezkiel	m
Ḥavah	Ḥavah	f
Ḥaval	Ḥavah	f
Ḥavala	Ḥavah	f
Ḥavaleh	Ḥavah	f
Ḥaveh	Ḥavah	f
Ḥavel	Ḥavah	f
Ḥavela	Ḥavah	f
Ḥaveleh	Ḥavah	f
Ḥavka	Ḥavah	f
Ḥavke	Ḥavah	f
Ḥayyim	Ḥayyim	m
Ḥayyiman	Ḥayyim	m
Ḥayyimel	Ḥayyim	m
Ḥayyimka	Ḥayyim	m
Ḥayyimke	Ḥayyim	m
Ḥeika	Ḥaiyyah	f
Ḥeikalle	Ḥaiyyah	f
Ḥeike	Ḥaiyyah	f
Ḥeikel	Ḥayyim	m
Ḥeikelle	Ḥaiyyah	f
Ḥeskel	Yeḥezkiel	m
Ḥiel	Yeḥiel	m
Ḥizkiyahu	Ḥizkiyahu	m
Ḥizkiyohu	Ḥizkiyahu	m
Ḥona	Yoḥanan	m
Ḥona	Elḥanan	m
Ḥone	Elḥanan	m
Ḥone	Yoḥanan	m
Ḥoni	Yoḥanan	m
Ḥoni	Elḥanan	m
Ḥonon	Elḥanan	m
Ḥonon	Yoḥanan	m
Icze	Yitzhak	m
Iddel	Yehudah	m
Idit	Yehudit	f
Igla	Avigaiyil	f
Igle	Avigaiyil	f
Ikh'l Mikh'l	Yeḥiel	m
Ikhal Mikhal	Mikhael	m
Ikhel	Yeḥiel	m
Ikhil	Yeḥiel	m
Ilka	Illa	f
Ilke	Illa	f
Illa	Illa	f
Illush	Illa	f
Iska	Yiskah	f
Iske	Yiskah	f
Isokhar	Yisakhar	m
Isokhor	Yisakhar	m
Isser	Yisrael	m
Isserel	Yisrael	m
Isserlein	Yisrael	m
Isserlin	Yisrael	m
Isserlis	Yisrael	m
Itka	Ester	f
Itka	Yehudit	f
Itke	Yehudit	f
Itke	Ester	f
Itta	Ester	f
Itta	Yehudit	f
Itte	Ester	f
Itte	Yehudit	f
Itzel	Yitzhak	m
Itzik	Yitzhak	m
Jonah	Jonah	f
Kalman	Kalonymus	m
Kalmenka	Kalonymus	m
Kalmenke	Kalonymus	m
Kalonymus	Kalonymus	m
Kashman	Yekutiel	m
Kassia	Ketziah	f
Kassie	Ketziah	f
Katzia	Ketziah	f
Katzie	Ketziah	f
Keika	Haiyyah	f
Keike	Haiyyah	f
Keikela	Haiyyah	f
Keikelle	Haiyyah	f
Keila	Haiyyah	f
Keile	Haiyyah	f
Kerpel	Yakov	m
Ketziah	Ketziah	f
Khassia	Ketziah	f

Name	Root Name	Sex
Khassie	Ketziah	f
Kooni	Kuni	m
Koppel	Yakov	m
Koppil	Yakov	m
Koppul	Yakov	m
Koshman	Yekutiel	m
Kosman	Yekutiel	m
Kovel	Yakov	m
Kovi	Yakov	m
Kozel	Yekutiel	m
Kozman	Yekutiel	m
Kuba	Yakov	m
Kube	Yakov	m
Kule	Yakov	m
Kuli	Yakov	m
Kuna	Kuni	m
Kuna	Kuna	f
Kune	Kuna	f
Kune	Kuni	m
Kuni	Kuni	m
Kunya	Kuni	m
Kunya	Kuna	f
Kunye	Kuna	f
Kunye	Kuni	m
Kuvel	Yakov	m
Lam	Lemuel	m
Lamlin	Lemuel	m
Lei'l	Leiah	f
Leiah	Leiah	f
Leiale	Leiah	f
Leib	Aryeh	m
Leibel	Aryeh	m
Leibele	Aryeh	m
Leibish	Aryeh	m
Leibush	Aryeh	m
Leicza	Leiah	f
Leicze	Leiah	f
Leika	Leiah	f
Leike	Leiah	f
Leima	Lemuel	m
Leiman	Lemuel	m
Leitza	Leiah	f
Leitze	Leiah	f
Leiyinka	Leiah	f
Leiyinke	Leiah	f
Leizer	Eliezer	m
Leizerel	Eliezer	m
Leizerke	Eliezer	m
Leizir	Eliezer	m
Leme	Lemuel	m
Lemekhel	Lemuel	m
Lemekhil	Lemuel	m
Lemel	Lemuel	m
Lemke	Lemuel	m
Lemken	Lemuel	m
Lemki	Lemuel	m
Lemkin	Lemuel	m
Lemla	Lemuel	m
Lemle	Lemuel	m
Lemlein	Lemuel	m
Lemlin	Lemuel	m
Lemoel	Lemuel	m
Lemuel	Lemuel	m
Lev	Aryeh	m
Levke	Aryeh	m
Liba	Lieba	f
Libbe	Lieba	f
Libbel	Lieba	f
Liber	Lieber	m
Liber'l	Lieber	m
Liberel	Lieba	f
Liberil	Lieba	f
Liberman	Lieber	m
Lieba	Lieba	f
Liebe	Lieba	f
Liebel	Lieba	f
Lieber	Lieber	m
Lieberman	Lieber	m
Liebman	Lieber	m
Lifsha	Lieba	f
Lifshe	Lieba	f
Lima	Lemuel	m
Liman	Lemuel	m
Lipka	Lieber	m
Lipke	Lieber	m
Lipman	Lieber	m
Lippa	Lieber	m
Lippe	Lieber	m
Lippman	Lieber	m
Lippmann	Lieber	m
Livsha	Lieba	f
Livshe	Lieba	f
Lozer	Elazar	m
Lozir	Elazar	m
Lozor	Elazar	m
Luba	Lieba	f
Maharam	Meir	m
Maḥlah	Maḥlah	f
Maḥle	Maḥlah	f
Mairem	Meir	m
Makhla	Maḥlah	f
Makhle	Maḥlah	f
Malkah	Malkah	f
Malkala	Malkah	f

Name	Root Name	Sex	Name	Root Name	Sex
Malkale	Malkah	f	Meishe	Moshe	m
Malkela	Malkah	f	Meishel	Moshe	m
Malkele	Malkah	f	Meishil	Moshe	m
Malya	Amelia	f	Meita	Matilda	f
Malye	Amelia	f	Meite	Matilda	f
Manish	Menashe	m	Melekh	Elimelekh	m
Mann	Menaḥem	m	Melikh	Elimelekh	m
Mannele	Menaḥem	m	Menaḥem	Menaḥem	m
Mannes	Menashe	m	Menashe	Menashe	m
Mannis	Menashe	m	Mendel	Menaḥem	m
Mannkhen	Menaḥem	m	Mendil	Menaḥem	m
Manuel	Emanuel	m	Mendl	Menaḥem	m
Manya	Emanuel	m	Meni	Emanuel	m
Maram	Meir	m	Menia	Menuḥah	f
Marem	Meir	m	Menie	Menuḥah	f
Margola	Margolah	f	Menka	Menaḥem	m
Margolah	Margolah	f	Menke	Menaḥem	m
Margoleh	Margolah	f	Menkhin	Menaḥem	m
Margolis	Margolah	f	Menni	Menaḥem	m
Margolit	Margolah	f	Menuḥah	Menuḥah	f
Margoliyah	Margolah	f	Merel	Miriam	f
Marim	Meir	m	Merele	Miriam	f
Mariyam	Miriam	f	Merka	Miriam	f
Mariyasha	Miriam Rachelle	f	Merke	Miriam	f
Mariyashe	Miriam Rachelle	f	Merkel	Miriam	f
Mariyashel	Miriam Rachelle	f	Meshel	Moshe	m
Mariyashil	Miriam Rachelle	f	Meshil	Moshe	m
Mariyashka	Miriam Rachelle	f	Meshka	Muskat	f
Mariyashke	Miriam Rachelle	f	Meshke	Muskat	f
Marum	Meir	m	Meshulam	Meshulam	m
Masha	Masheh	f	Mikhael	Mikhael	m
Mashah	Masheh	f	Mikhal	Mikhael	m
Mashe	Masheh	f	Mikhlin	Mikhael	m
Masheh	Masheh	f	Mikhoel	Mikhael	m
Mata	Matrona	f	Mina	Menuhah	f
Matel	Matrona	f	Mindel	Menuhah	f
Matela	Matrona	f	Mindil	Menuhah	f
Mateleh	Matrona	f	Mindul	Menuhah	f
Matil	Matrona	f	Minka	Menuhah	f
Matilda	Matilda	f	Minke	Menuhah	f
Matrona	Matrona	f	Minneh	Menuhah	f
Matte	Matrona	f	Mira	Miriam	f
Mazal	Mazal	f	Mireh	Miriam	f
Meidlin	Matilda	f	Mirel	Miriam	f
Meilekh	Elimelekh	m	Mirela	Miriam	f
Meilikh	Elimelekh	m	Mirele	Miriam	f
Meir	Meir	m	Miriam	Miriam	f
Meiram	Meir	m	Miriam Rachelle	Miriam Rachelle	f
Meirel	Meir	m	Mirka	Miriam	f
Meiril	Meir	m	Mirke	Miriam	f
Meirke	Meir	m	Moddel	Mordekhai	m
Meisha	Moshe	m	Moishe	Moshe	m

Name	Root Name	Sex
Monash	Menashe	m
Monel	Emanuel	m
Moni	Emanuel	m
Monish	Menashe	m
Monnis	Menashe	m
Monoil	Emanuel	m
Monya	Emanuel	m
Monye	Emanuel	m
Mordekhai	Mordekhai	m
Mordel	Mordekhai	m
Mordush	Mordekhai	m
Morkel	Mordekhai	m
Morkil	Mordekhai	m
Morkl	Mordekhai	m
Moshe	Moshe	m
Moshka	Moshe	m
Moshke	Moshe	m
Motka	Mordekhai	m
Motke	Mordekhai	m
Motta	Mordekhai	m
Motte	Mordekhai	m
Mottel	Mordekhai	m
Mulik	Shmuel	m
Mulka	Shmuel	m
Mulke	Shmuel	m
Muna	Menuhah	f
Munczia	Menahem	m
Mune	Menuhah	f
Munia	Menuhah	f
Munie	Menuhah	f
Mushka	Muskat	f
Mushke	Muskat	f
Muska	Muskat	f
Muskat	Muskat	f
Muskatel	Muskat	f
Muske	Muskat	f
Naftali	Naftali	m
Naftoli	Naftali	m
Naftoli Hertz	Naftali	m
Nahalah	Nahalah	f
Nakha	Nahalah	f
Nakhe	Nahalah	f
Nakhla	Nahalah	f
Nakhle	Nahalah	f
Nakhli	Nahalah	f
Nasanel	Natanel	m
Natan	Natan	m
Natanel	Natanel	m
Natty	Naftali	m
Nehomah	Neḥamah	f
Neḥamah	Neḥamah	f
Neḥamel	Neḥamah	f
Neḥamka	Neḥamah	f
Neḥamke	Neḥamah	f
Nekha	Neḥamah	f
Nekhe	Neḥamah	f
Nekhel	Neḥamah	f
Nina	Peninah	f
Ninneh	Peninah	f
Nossel	Natan	m
Nosson Notta	Natan	m
Nosson Notte	Natan	m
Nosson	Natan	m
Notinka	Natan	m
Notinke	Natan	m
Notka	Natan	m
Notke	Natan	m
Notta	Natan	m
Notte	Natan	m
Nottel	Natan	m
Nottele	Natan	m
Ogla	Avigaiyil	f
Ogle	Avigaiyil	f
Oglin	Avigaiyil	f
Ogush	Avigaiyil	f
Ogushe	Avigaiyil	f
Orcze	Uri	m
Ore	Aharon	m
Orel	Aharon	m
Oren	Aharon	m
Orke	Aharon	m
Orlik	Uri	m
Orush	Aharon	m
Osher	Asher	m
Osher'l	Asher	m
Osherel	Asher	m
Osnas	Asnat	f
Pai'ah	Puah	f
Pai'eh	Puah	f
Paika	Puah	f
Paike	Puah	f
Pasha	Batyah	f
Pashe	Batyah	f
Pei'ah	Puah	f
Pei'al	Puah	f
Pei'ale	Puah	f
Pei'eh	Puah	f
Pei'el	Puah	f
Pei'ele	Puah	f
Peninah	Peninah	f
Perel	Peninah	f
Perele	Peninah	f
Perril	Peninah	f
Pesa	Batyah	f

Name	Root Name	Sex
Pese	Batyah	f
Pesha	Batyah	f
Peshe	Batyah	f
Peshya	Batyah	f
Peshye	Batyah	f
Pesya	Batyah	f
Pesye	Batyah	f
Pinhas	Pinhas	m
Pinhas'l	Pinhas	m
Pinna	Pinhas	m
Pinne	Pinhas	m
Pinnel	Pinhas	m
Pinya	Pinhas	m
Pinye	Pinhas	m
Puah	Puah	f
Raḥel	Raḥel	f
Rafael	Rafael	m
Rasha	Raḥel	f
Rashe	Raḥel	f
Rashel	Raḥel	f
Rashi	Raḥel	f
Rashil	Raḥel	f
Rashka	Raḥel	f
Rashke	Raḥel	f
Rasi	Raḥel	f
Rasia	Raḥel	f
Rasie	Raḥel	f
Raska	Raḥel	f
Raske	Raḥel	f
Reddel	Roda	f
Reiḥil	Raḥel	f
Reitza	Roza	f
Reitze	Roza	f
Reitzel	Roza	f
Reiyelina	Raḥel	f
Reiza	Roza	f
Reizeh	Roza	f
Reizel	Roza	f
Reizil	Roza	f
Rekel	Raḥel	f
Rekha	Raḥel	f
Rekhe	Raḥel	f
Rela	Raḥel	f
Releh	Raḥel	f
Relin	Raḥel	f
Rikel	Raḥel	f
Rikla	Raḥel	f
Rikle	Raḥel	f
Risha	Raḥel	f
Rishe	Raḥel	f
Ritl	Ruth	f
Ritla	Ruth	f
Ritleh	Ruth	f
Rittel	Ruth	f
Riva	Rivkah	f
Rivah	Rivkah	f
Riveh	Rivkah	f
Rivel	Rivkah	f
Rivkah	Rivkah	f
Rivke	Rivkah	f
Rivkela	Rivkah	f
Rivkele	Rivkah	f
Rivlin	Rivkah	f
Rizil	Roza	f
Roda	Roda	f
Rodde	Roda	f
Rodel	Roda	f
Rodka	Roda	f
Rodke	Roda	f
Roḥel	Raḥel	f
Roiza	Roza	f
Roizeh	Roza	f
Rokha	Rahel	f
Rokhale	Rahel	f
Rokhe	Rahel	f
Rokhele	Rahel	f
Rokhlin	Rahel	f
Rossa	Roza	f
Rosseh	Roza	f
Roza	Roza	f
Rozeh	Roza	f
Rus	Ruth	f
Rushka	Roza	f
Rushke	Roza	f
Rut	Ruth	f
Ruth	Ruth	f
Rutl	Ruth	f
Rutul	Ruth	f
Sabatka	Sabta	f
Sabatke	Sabta	f
Sabatki	Sabta	f
Sabta	Sabta	f
Salida	Salida	f
Sander	Aleksander	m
Sandor	Aleksander	m
Sandush	Aleksander	m
Sanel	Natanel	m
Sanne	Natanel	m
Sarah	Sarah	f
Sekel	Yitzhak	m
Sender	Aleksander	m
Sender'l	Aleksander	m
Sendush	Aleksander	m
Serrel	Sarah	f

Name	Root Name	Sex
Serril	Sarah	f
Sha'oil	Sha'ul	m
Sha'ul	Sha'ul	m
Shabsel	Shabtai	m
Shabsi	Shabtai	m
Shabsil	Shabtai	m
Shabtai	Shabtai	m
Shabtel	Shabtai	m
Shabtil	Shabtai	m
Shaika	Yeshaiyahu	m
Shaike	Yeshaiyahu	m
Shaiya	Yeshaiyahu	m
Shakhna	Shakhna	m
Shakhne	Shakhna	m
Shalom	Meshulam	m
Shalom	Shalom	m
Shalom Shakhna	Shakhna	m
Shaptaiyah	Shaptaiyah	m
Shebtel	Shabtai	m
Shebtil	Shabtai	m
Sheima	Shimon	m
Sheime	Shimon	m
Sheina	Yaffah	f
Sheindel	Yaffah	f
Sheindele	Yaffah	f
Sheindil	Yaffah	f
Sheine	Yaffah	f
Shekhna	Shakhna	m
Shekhne	Shakhna	m
Shepsel	Shabtai	m
Shepsil	Shabtai	m
Shept'l	Shaptaiyah	m
Sheptel	Shabtai	m
Sheptel	Shaptaiyah	m
Sheptil	Shaptaiyah	m
Sheptil	Shabtai	m
Shil'm	Meshulam	m
Shimon	Shimon	m
Shimonel	Shimon	m
Shimonka	Shimon	m
Shimonke	Shimon	m
Shlemiel	Shlumiel	m
Shloimah	Shlomoh	m
Shlomel	Shlomoh	m
Shlomiel	Shlumiel	m
Shlomka	Shlomoh	m
Shlomke	Shlomoh	m
Shlomoh	Shlomoh	m
Shlomoh Zalman	Shlomoh	m
Shlumiel	Shlumiel	m
Shmaryah	Shmaryahu	m
Shmaryahu	Shmaryahu	m

Name	Root Name	Sex
Shmelka	Shmuel	m
Shmelke	Shmuel	m
Shmer'l	Shmaryahu	m
Shmerel	Shmaryahu	m
Shmeril	Shmaryahu	m
Shmerlein	Shmaryahu	m
Shmerlin	Shmaryahu	m
Shmuel	Shmuel	m
Shmulik	Shmuel	m
Shmulka	Shmuel	m
Shmulke	Shmuel	m
Shnaiya	Sinai	m
Shnaiye	Sinai	m
Shnei'or	Shnei'or	m
Shnei'or Zalman	Shnei'or	m
Shnei'ur Zalman	Shnei'or	m
Shner	Shnei'or	m
Shoi'el	Sha'ul	m
Shoi'l	Sha'ul	m
Sholikeh	Sha'ul	m
Sholom	Meshulam	m
Sholom	Shalom	m
Sholom Shakhna	Shakhna	m
Shosha	Shoshanah	f
Shoshanah	Shoshanah	f
Shoshe	Shoshanah	f
Shoshel	Shoshanah	f
Shoshka	Shoshanah	f
Shoshke	Shoshanah	f
Shprintza	Tikvah	f
Shprintzak	Tikvah	f
Shprintze	Tikvah	f
Shprintzel	Tikvah	f
Shprintzik	Tikvah	f
Shraga Feivush	Shraga Feivush	m
Shula	Shulamit	f
Shulam	Meshulam	m
Shulamis	Shulamit	f
Shulamit	Shulamit	f
Shuleh	Shulamit	f
Shulka	Shulamit	f
Shulke	Shulamit	f
Shulman	Meshulam	m
Shulom	Shalom	m
Shushanah	Shoshanah	f
Sima	Simhah	f
Simhah	Simhah	f
Simka	Simhah	f
Simkeh	Simhah	f
Simmeh	Simhah	f
Sinai	Sinai	m
Sinaiya	Sinai	m

Name	Root Name	Sex
Sinaiye	Sinai	m
Sirka	Sarah	f
Sirke	Sarah	f
Sirki	Sarah	f
Sirrel	Sarah	f
Sirril	Sarah	f
Sitta	Tzitta	f
Sitte	Tzitta	f
Sittel	Tzitta	f
Sittil	Tzitta	f
Sob'l	Sabta	f
Soba	Sabta	f
Sobel	Sabta	f
Sol	Malkah	f
Sorah	Sarah	f
Sorka	Sarah	f
Sorke	Sarah	f
Sorkel	Sarah	f
Sorkil	Sarah	f
Sorrel	Sarah	f
Sorril	Sarah	f
Srol	Yisrael	m
Sroli	Yisrael	m
Srolik	Yisrael	m
Srolka	Yisrael	m
Srolke	Yisrael	m
Srul	Yisrael	m
Sruli	Yisrael	m
Srulik	Yisrael	m
Srulka	Yisrael	m
Srulke	Yisrael	m
Sterel	Ester	f
Sterlein	Ester	f
Sterlin	Ester	f
Sterna	Ester	f
Sterne	Ester	f
Sul	Malkah	f
Sultana	Malkah	f
Tamar	Tamar	f
Tamarah	Tamar	f
Tamarka	Tamar	f
Tamarke	Tamar	f
Te'bil	Yonah	f
Tehillah	Tehillah	f
Teib'l	Yonah	f
Teib'l	Jonah	f
Teiba	Jonah	f
Teiba	Yonah	f
Teibe	Yonah	f
Teibe	Jonah	f
Teibel	Jonah	f
Teibel	Yonah	f
Teibil	Jonah	f
Temel	Tamar	f
Temer	Tamar	f
Temerel	Tamar	f
Temeril	Tamar	f
Temka	Tamar	f
Temke	Tamar	f
Temma	Tamar	f
Temmeh	Tamar	f
Tev	Tuvyah	m
Teve	Tuvyah	m
Tevel	David	m
Tevel	Tuvyah	m
Tevele	David	m
Tevele	Tuvyah	m
Tevil	David	m
Tevil	Tuvyah	m
Tevya	Tuvyah	m
Tevye	Tuvyah	m
Theodoros	Theodoros	m
Tikvah	Tikvah	f
Tilka	Tehillah	f
Tilkeh	Tehillah	f
Tilla	Tehillah	f
Tilleh	Tehillah	f
Tirtzah	Tirtzah	f
Tirtze	Tirtzah	f
Tirtzel	Tirtzah	f
Todras	Theodoros	m
Todres	Theodoros	m
Todris	Theodoros	m
Todros	Theodoros	m
Toiba	Yonah	f
Toiba	Jonah	f
Toibe	Yonah	f
Toibe	Jonah	f
Tolli	Naftali	m
Tovah	Tovah	f
Tovel	Tovah	f
Treina	Ester	f
Treindel	Ester	f
Treine	Ester	f
Trina	Ester	f
Trinne	Ester	f
Tuvyah	Tuvyah	m
Tzale	Betzalel	m
Tzalel	Betzalel	m
Tzalka	Betzalel	m
Tzalke	Betzalel	m
Tzarina	Czarna	f
Tzarine	Czarna	f
Tzarna	Czarna	f

Name	Root Name	Sex
Tzarne	Czarna	f
Tzeitlin	Tzitta	f
Tzeitta	Tzitta	f
Tzeitte	Tzitta	f
Tzeittel	Tzitta	f
Tzeittil	Tzitta	f
Tzipka	Tzipporah	f
Tzipke	Tzipporah	f
Tzippa	Tzipporah	f
Tzippe	Tzipporah	f
Tzipporah	Tzipporah	f
Tzira	Tzireh	f
Tzireh	Tzireh	f
Tzirel	Tzireh	f
Tzirele	Tzireh	f
Tziril	Tzireh	f
Tzirka	Tzireh	f
Tzirke	Tzireh	f
Tzitta	Tzitta	f
Tzitte	Tzitta	f
Tzittel	Tzitta	f
Tzittil	Tzitta	f
Tziviah	Tzviah	f
Tzvi	Tzvi	m
Tzviah	Tzviah	f
Ulli	Yisrael	m
Ure	Uri	m
Urele	Uri	m
Uri	Uri	m
Veibish	Shraga Feivush	m
Veibush	Shraga Feivush	m
Veira	Devorah	f
Veire	Devorah	f
Veish'l	Efraiyim	m
Velka	Zeev	m
Velke	Zeev	m
Velvel	Zeev	m
Velvele	Zeev	m
Vera	Devorah	f
Vidal	Ḥayyim	m
Vish'l	Efraiyim	m
Vital	Ḥayyim	m
Volf	Zeev	m
Volvel	Zeev	m
Vulf	Zeev	m
Wolf	Zeev	m
Wulf	Zeev	m
Yaffah	Yaffah	f
Yaffeh	Yaffah	f
Yakhe	Yokheved	f
Yakhna	Yoḥanah	f
Yakhne	Yoḥanah	f

Name	Root Name	Sex
Yakov	Yakov	m
Yankel	Yakov	m
Yankele	Yakov	m
Yedidiah	Gottlieb	m
Yedidyah	Gottlieb	m
Yehezkiel	Yehezkiel	m
Yehoishua	Yehoshua	m
Yehoshua	Yehoshua	m
Yehoshua Folk	Yehoshua	m
Yehuda	Yehudah	m
Yehudah	Yehudah	m
Yehudah Leib	Yehudah	m
Yehudah Yudel	Yehudah	m
Yehudis	Yehudit	f
Yehudit	Yehudit	f
Yeḥiel	Yeḥiel	m
Yeina	Yonah	f
Yeine	Yonah	f
Yeino	Yonah	f
Yekel	Yakov	m
Yekil	Yakov	m
Yekusiel	Yekutiel	m
Yekutiel	Yekutiel	m
Yenta	Gentille	f
Yente	Gentille	f
Yentel	Gentille	f
Yenteleh	Gentille	f
Yentileh	Gentille	f
Yentlin	Gentille	f
Yeshaiya	Yeshaiyahu	m
Yeshaiyahu	Yeshaiyahu	m
Yeshaiyohu	Yeshaiyahu	m
Yessel	Yosef	m
Yessil	Yosef	m
Yiddel	Yehudah	m
Yisakhar	Yisakhar	m
Yiskah	Yiskah	f
Yiskoh	Yiskah	f
Yisokhar	Yisakhar	m
Yisokhor Berman	Yisakhar	m
Yisokhor	Yisakhar	m
Yisokhor Ber	Yisakhar	m
Yisrael	Yisrael	m
Yisroel	Yisrael	m
Yisrol	Yisrael	m
Yitta	Yehudit	f
Yitte	Yehudit	f
Yittel	Yehudit	f
Yitzhak	Yitzhak	m
Yitzhok	Yitzhak	m
Yoḥanah	Yoḥanah	f
Yoḥanan	Yoḥanan	m

Name	Root Name	Sex
Yoḥanon	Yoḥanan	m
Yoḥonon	Yoḥanan	m
Yoina	Yonah	f
Yoine	Yonah	f
Yoino	Yonah	f
Yokel	Yakov	m
Yokha	Yokheved	f
Yokhe	Yokheved	f
Yokheved	Yokheved	f
Yoki	Elyakim	m
Yokil	Yakov	m
Yokim	Elyakim	m
Yokum	Elyakim	m
Yonah	Yonah	f
Yosef Yoske	Yosef	m
Yosef	Yosef	m
Yoshka	Yosef	m
Yoshke	Yosef	m
Yoska	Yosef	m
Yoske	Yosef	m
Yossel	Yosef	m
Yozpa	Yosef	m
Yozpe	Yosef	m
Yuda	Yehudah	m
Yude	Yehudah	m
Yudel	Yehudah	m
Yudit	Yehudit	f
Yudit'l	Yehudit	f
Yutka	Yehudah	m
Yutke	Yehudah	m
Yutta	Yehudit	f
Yutte	Yehudit	f
Yuttel	Yehudit	f
Yuttele	Yehudit	f
Yuzpa	Yosef	m
Yuzpe	Yosef	m
Zale	Betzalel	m
Zalel	Betzalel	m
Zalka	Betzalel	m
Zalke	Betzalel	m
Zalman	Shlomoh	m
Zalmanka	Shlomoh	m
Zalmanke	Shlomoh	m
Zalmina	Shlomoh	m
Zaman'l	Shlomoh	m
Zanvil	Shmuel	m
Zavel	Shmuel	m
Zavil	Shmuel	m
Zeev	Zeev	m
Zeev Wolf	Zeev	m
Zeida	Zeide	m
Zeide	Zeide	m
Zeidel	Zeide	m
Zeidil	Zeide	m
Zeidl	Zeide	m
Zekel	Yitzhak	m
Zelda	Salida	f
Zelde	Salida	f
Zelig	Zelig	m
Zeligman	Zelig	m
Zelikman	Zelig	m
Zelle	Zelig	m
Zelman	Shlomoh	m
Zelmen	Shlomoh	m
Zelmina	Shlomoh	m
Zimmel	Shimon	m
Zimmil	Shimon	m
Zimmul	Shimon	m
Zissa	Zissa	f
Zissa	Zussman	m
Zisse	Zussman	m
Zisse	Zissa	f
Zissel	Zussman	m
Zissel	Zissa	f
Zissil	Zissa	f
Zlota	Golda	f
Zlotte	Golda	f
Zundel	Zundel	m
Zundil	Zundel	m
Zundul	Zundel	m
Zusha	Zussman	m
Zushe	Zussman	m
Zushel	Zussman	m
Zushia	Zussman	m
Zushie	Zussman	m
Zussa	Zussman	m
Zusse	Zussman	m
Zussia	Zussman	m
Zussie	Zussman	m
Zussman	Zussman	m

Family Names Derived From Diminutive Forms Dealt Within This Book

Name	Root Name	Sex
Abeles	Avraham	m
Abelesz	Abraham	m
Aizikman	Yitzḥak	m
Aizman	Yitzḥak	m
Alter	Alter	m
Altman	Alter	m
Batkin	Batyah	f
Berkowitz	Dov	m
Berlin	Dov	m
Bloom	Shoshanah	f
Blum	Shoshanah	f
Culi	Yakov	m
Cunin	Kuna	f
Dobkin	Dobah	f
Dobrushkin	Tovah	f
Dvorkin	Devorah	f
Elkin	Illa	f
Elkind	Illa	f
Eskin	Ester	f
Etkin	Ester	f
Feigin	Tzipporah	f
Feiglin	Tzipporah	f
Fogel	Tzipporah	f
Fradkin	Freida	f
Freidkin	Freida	f
Frumkin	Frommet	f
Getz	Gottschalk	m
Gishin	Gisse	f
Gissin	Gisse	f
Glickman	Mazal	f
Glicksman	Mazal	f
Gluckman	Mazal	f
Glucksman	Mazal	f
Goetz	Gottschalk	m
Gottlieb	Gottlieb	m
Gottschalk	Gottschalk	m
Groner	Gruna	f
Gulkes	Yakov	m
Gulkin	Yakov	m
Gulko	Yakov	m
Gutman	Toviyah	m
Ḥaikin	Ḥaiyyah	f
Ḥannales	Ḥannah	f
Havin	Ḥavah	f
Havkin	Ḥavah	f
Havlin	Ḥavah	f
Haskel	Yeḥezkiel	m
Haskil	Yeḥezkiel	m
Haskin	Ketziah	f
Ḥeikin	Ḥayyah	f
Heiman	Ḥayyim	m
Heller	Gelleh	f
Hendel	Ḥanokh	m
Hendil	Ḥanokh	m
Hendl	Ḥanokh	m
Herschel	Tzvi	m
Heschel	Yehoshua	m
Hess	Ḥizkiyahu	m
Heyman	Ḥayyim	m
Hirsch	Tzvi	m
Hirschel	Tzvi	m
Isserlein	Yisrael	m
Isserles	Yisrael	m
Isserlin	Yisrael	m
Jaffe	Yaffah	f
Jesselson	Yosef	m
Joffa	Yaffah	f
Joffe	Yaffah	f
Joskewitz	Yosef	m
Josselson	Yosef	m
Kashman	Yekutiel	m
Katzin	Ketziah	f
Kishin	Gisse	f
Koppel	Yakov	m
Kosman	Yekutiel	m
Kozman	Yekutiel	m
Kuli	Yakov	m
Kunin	Kuna	f
Lam	Lemuel	m
Leikin	Leiah	f
Leiman	Lemuel	m
Lieber	Lieber	m
Lieberman	Lieber	m
Liebman	Lieber	m

Name	Root Name	Sex
Liber	Lieber	m
Liberman	Lieber	m
Lipkin	Lieber	m
Lipman	Lieber	m
Lippman	Lieber	m
Lippmann	Lieber	m
Machles	Maḥlah	f
Machlis	Maḥlah	f
Maisel	Moshe	m
Maislish	Moshe	m
Maizel	Moshe	m
Makhles	Maḥlah	f
Makhlis	Maḥlah	f
Mandelbaum	Manaḥem	m
Mann	Menaḥem	m
Mannes	Menashe	m
Margolies	Margolah	f
Margoliot	Margolah	f
Margolioth	Margolah	f
Meisel	Moshe	m
Meisels	Moshe	m
Meizel	Moshe	m
Mendelbaum	Menaḥem	m
Menuḥin	Menuḥah	f
Merkel	Miriam	f
Merkes	Miriam	f
Merkil	Miriam	f
Merkin	Miriam	f
Merl	Miriam	f
Merlin	Miriam	f
Mindlin	Menuḥah	f
Mireles	Miriam	f
Mirelis	Miriam	f
Mirkes	Miriam	f
Mirkin	Miriam	f
Mirkis	Miriam	f
Monash	Menashe	m
Moscowitz	Moshe	m
Moshkowitz	Moshe	m
Muskat	Muskat	f
Naftolis	Naftoli	m
Naḥamkin	Neḥamah	f
Natkin	Natan	m
Nossell	Natan	m
Notkin	Natan	m

Name	Root Name	Sex
Ogushewitz	Avigaiyil	f
Ogushwitz	Avigaiyil	f
Orenstein	Uri	m
Paikowitz	Puah	f
Paikus	Puah	f
Paneth	Barukh	m
Patkin	Batyah	f
Peikowitz	Puah	f
Perlov	Peninah	f
Perlow	Peninah	f
Pikus	Puah	f
Pincus	Pinḥas	m
Pinkus	Pinḥas	m
Rashkin	Raḥel	f
Raskin	Raḥel	f
Redlich	Roda	f
Reizes	Roza	f
Rivkes	Rivkah	f
Rivkin	Rivkah	f
Rivkind	Rivkah	f
Rivlin	Rivkah	f
Rochlin	Raḥel	f
Rodkevitch	Roda	f
Rodkin	Roda	f
Roizes	Roza	f
Sabatka	Sabta	f
Sabatke	Sabta	f
Sabatki	Sabta	f
Sanders	Alexander	m
Saunders	Alexander	m
Scheiner	Yaffah	f
Schindel	Yaffah	f
Schindler	Yaffah	f
Schindling	Yaffah	f
Schöner	Yaffah	f
Seide	Zeide	m
Seidel	Zeide	m
Serkin	Sarah	f
Serlin	Sarah	f
Shaikevitz	Yeshaiyahu	m
Shaiyevitz	Yeshaiyahu	m
Shmerling	Shmaryahu	m
Shprintzak	Tikvah	f
Shulkin	Shulamit	f
Shulman	Meshulam	m

Name	Root Name	Sex
Sichel	Yitzḥak	m
Simkin	Simḥah	f
Sobel	Sabta	f
Sterling	Ester	f
Tamarkin	Tamar	f
Temkin	Tamar	f
Tilkin	Tehillah	f
Tilles	Tehillah	f
Tillis	Tehillah	f
Todras	Theodorus	m
Todres	Theodorus	m
Todris	Theodorus	m
Todros	Theodorus	m
Trainer	Ester	f
Treiner	Ester	f
Tumarkin	Tamar	f
Tzeitlin	Tzitta	f
Tzipkin	Tzipporah	f
Tzippin	Tzipporah	f
Tzirkin	Tzirah	f
Tzirkind	Tzirah	f
Vogel	Tzipporah	f
Wolf	Zeev	m
Yaffe	Yaffah	f
Yaffin	Yaffah	f
Yesselson	Yosef	m
Yoffa	Yaffah	f
Yoffe	Yaffah	f
Yoffin	Yaffah	f
Yoskewitz	Yosef	m
Yosselson	Yosef	m
Zeitlin	Tzitta	f
Zekel	Yitzḥak	m
Zeligman	Zelig	m
Zelminkas	Zalman	m
Zelminkes	Zalman	m
Zichel	Yitzḥak	m
Zimmel	Shimon	m
Zirkin	Tzirah	f
Zirkind	Tzirah	f
Zislin	Zissa	f

Additional Family Name Derivatives

Name	Root Name	Sex
Alexander	Aleksander	m
Altar	Alter	m
Alter	Alter	m
Arkin	Aharon	m
Beilin	Bilhah	f
Belkin	Bilhah	f
Devorkes	Devorah	f
Edels	Adinah	f
Eidels	Adinah	f
Falk	Refa'eil	m
Faitelovitch	Ḥayyim	m
Faitlovitch	Ḥayyim	m
Fish	Efrayim	m
Fishel	Efrayim	m
Fradkes	Freida	f
Freedman	Frieda	f
Freides	Freida	f
Freidin	Freida	f
Freidkes	Freida	f
Freidlin	Freida	f
Friedman	Frieda	f
Frumkes	Frommet	f
Gendel	Genana	f
Gutman	Toviyah	m
Ḥaikel	Ḥayyim	m
Ḥeikel	Ḥayyim	m
Handelman	Ḥanokh	m
Hendel	Tziviah	f
Hendel	Ḥanokh	m
Hendelman	Ḥanokh	m
Henkin	Ḥannah	f
Henschel	Asher	m
Henshel	Asher	m
Henzel	Asher	m
Henzil	Asher	m
Kalminkes	Kalonymus	m
Kaufman	Yaakov	m
Koppelman	Yaakov	m
Lamm	Lemu'eil	m
Leeman	Aryeih	m
Lehman	Aryeih	m
Leibler	Aryeih	m
Leikes	Lei'ah	f
Lipkes	Lieber	m
Lipsky	Lieber	m
Löbel	Aryeih	m
Loebel	Aryeih	m
Loewe	Aryeih	m
Löwe	Aryeih	m
Malkin	Malkah	f
Menkin	Menuḥah	f
Minkes	Menuḥah	f
Minkin	Menuḥah	f
Minkis	Menuḥah	f
Mushin	Masha	f
Neḥamkin	Neḥamah	f
Orkin	Aharon	m
Pereles	Peninah	f
Perels	Peninah	f
Perl	Peninah	f
Perlin	Peninah	f
Perlman	Peninah	f
Schwartz	Breina	f
Schwartzman	Breina	f
Schwarz	Breina	f
Schwarzman	Breina	f
Seelig	Asher	m
Seligman	Asher	m
Selikman	Asher	m
Shaḥor	Breina	f
Sirkes	Sarah	f
Slotkin	Golda	f
Suuskind	Zussya	m
Sussman	Zussya	m
Veit	Ḥayyim	m
Vidal	Ḥayyim	m
Vital	Ḥayyim	m
Wolpe	Ze'eiv	m
Wolper	Ze'eiv	m
Wolfish	Ze'eiv	m
Yankelevitch	Yaakov	m
Zabel	Shmu'eil	m
Zalkin	Betzaleil	m
Zalkind	Betzaleil	m
Zeligman	Asher	m
Zelikman	Asher	m
Zelkin	Betzaleil	m
Zelkind	Betzaleil	m
Zichlin	Yitzḥak	m
Ziskind	Zussya	m
Zlotkin	Golda	m
Zussman	Zussya	m